DATE DUE

JAN 2 2 2009		
MAR 03		

HIGHSMITH #45115

THE AIR FORCE IN ACTION

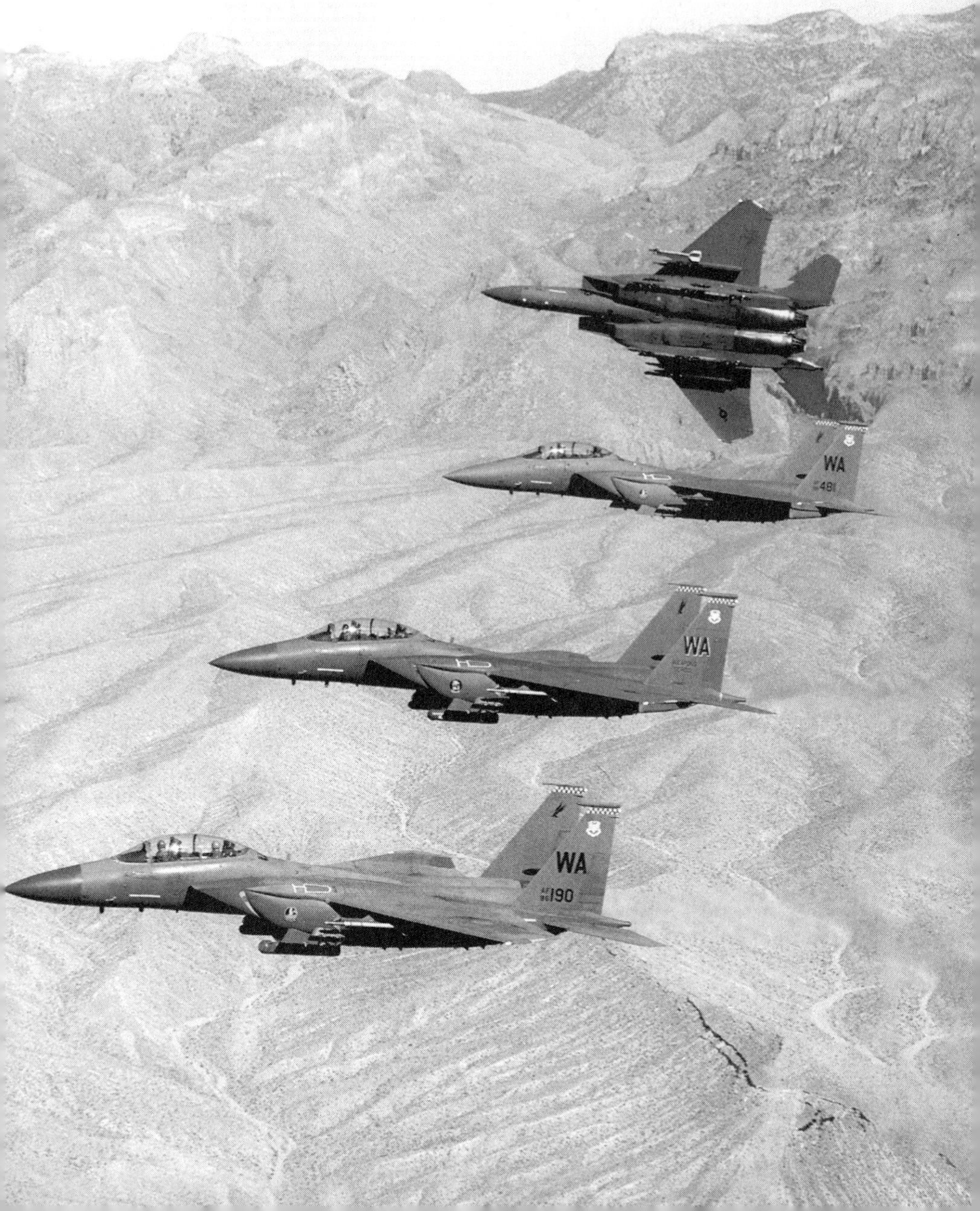

Titles in *U.S. Military Branches and Careers*

The Air Force in Action
ISBN 0-7660-1636-6

The Army in Action
ISBN 0-7660-1635-8

The Coast Guard in Action
ISBN 0-7660-1634-X

The Marine Corps in Action
ISBN 0-7660-1637-4

The Navy in Action
ISBN 0-7660-1633-1

U.S. Military Branches and Careers

THE AIR FORCE in ACTION

Hill Middle School LMC
1836 Brookdale Road
Naperville, IL 60563

Wanda Langley

3001100018237

Enslow Publishers, Inc.

40 Industrial Road   PO Box 38
Box 398   Aldershot
Berkeley Heights, NJ 07922   Hants GU12 6BP
USA   UK
http://www.enslow.com

Library of Congress Cataloging-in-Publication Data

Langley, Wanda.
    The Air Force in action / Wanda Langley.
        p. cm. — (U.S. military branches and careers)
    Includes bibliographical references and index.
    ISBN 0-7660-1636-6
    1. United States. Air Force—Vocational guidance—Juvenile literature.
[1. United States. Air Force. 2. United States. Air Force—Vocational
guidance. 3. Vocational guidance.] I. Title. II. Series.
    UG633 .L263 2001
    358.4'0023'73—dc21

                                                            2001000312

Printed in the United States of America

10 9 8 7 6 5 4 3 2

To Our Readers: We have done our best to make sure all Internet addresses in
this book were active and appropriate when we went to press. However, the
author and the publisher have no control over and assume no liability for the
material available on those Internet sites or on other Web sites they may link to.
Any comments or suggestions can be sent by e-mail to comments@enslow.com or
to the address on the back cover.

Illustration Credits: All photos are courtesy U.S. Department of
Defense, except for the following: U.S. Air Force, pp. 11, 15, 48, 50, 51,
78, 81, 105, 107, 117; National Archives, pp. 20–21, 23, 25, 27, 31, 32,
34, 36, 98, 102; NASA, pp. 38, 40; U.S. Air Force Academy, p. 59;
Corel Corp., p. 61; San Diego Aerospace Museum, p. 100; Library of
Congress, p. 108.

Cover Illustrations: U.S. Air Force (background); U. S. Department of
Defense (inset).

U.S. Military Branches and Careers

THE AIR FORCE IN ACTION

Hill Middle School LMC
1836 Brookdale Road
Naperville, IL 60563

Wanda Langley

3001100018237

Enslow Publishers, Inc.

40 Industrial Road	PO Box 38
Box 398	Aldershot
Berkeley Heights, NJ 07922	Hants GU12 6BP
USA	UK

http://www.enslow.com

Library of Congress Cataloging-in-Publication Data

Langley, Wanda.
    The Air Force in action / Wanda Langley.
       p. cm. — (U.S. military branches and careers)
    Includes bibliographical references and index.
    ISBN 0-7660-1636-6
    1. United States. Air Force—Vocational guidance—Juvenile literature.
[1. United States. Air Force. 2. United States. Air Force—Vocational
guidance. 3. Vocational guidance.] I. Title. II. Series.
UG633 .L263 2001
358.4'0023'73—dc21
                                   2001000312

Printed in the United States of America

10 9 8 7 6 5 4 3 2

To Our Readers: We have done our best to make sure all Internet addresses in this book were active and appropriate when we went to press. However, the author and the publisher have no control over and assume no liability for the material available on those Internet sites or on other Web sites they may link to. Any comments or suggestions can be sent by e-mail to comments@enslow.com or to the address on the back cover.

Illustration Credits: All photos are courtesy U.S. Department of Defense, except for the following: U.S. Air Force, pp. 11, 15, 48, 50, 51, 78, 81, 105, 107, 117; National Archives, pp. 20–21, 23, 25, 27, 31, 32, 34, 36, 98, 102; NASA, pp. 38, 40; U.S. Air Force Academy, p. 59; Corel Corp., p. 61; San Diego Aerospace Museum, p. 100; Library of Congress, p. 108.

Cover Illustrations: U.S. Air Force (background); U. S. Department of Defense (inset).

Contents

The Mission of Today's Air Force

During the winter and spring of 1999, thousands of people fled the province of Kosovo, a part of Serbia in the southeastern European country of Yugoslavia. They were citizens of Kosovo, but their ethnic background was Albanian. The president of Yugoslavia, Slobodan Milosevic, had ordered the removal of all ethnic Albanians from Kosovo. The Yugoslav military and Serbian special police burned homes and shot defenseless people in the effort to drive them out. Armed Serbian police loaded the people on trains, tractors, and even horse-drawn carts. Others fled on foot, carrying their few possessions or taking just the clothes on their backs. Four hundred fifty thousand men, women, and children streamed toward neighboring countries, seeking refuge.

People around the world became aware of what was happening and responded. The United States and its military allies in Europe, which together make up the North Atlantic Treaty Organization (NATO), launched

Three F-4 airplanes from the 561st Fighter Wing, Nellis Air Force Base, Nevada, fly over the Mediterranean Sea and Saudi Arabia. Fighter planes were used to patrol the skies over Kosovo as part of the NATO effort to restore peace to the region.

air strikes against Serbia to stop the atrocities, and world relief organizations worked together to send food and other supplies.

America's contribution to this humanitarian effort was Joint Task Force (JTF) Shining Hope, made up of units from the Air Force, Army, Navy, and Marines. The United States Air Force had the principal responsibility of airlifting supplies to the refugees. Air Force Major General William Hinton, Jr., directed this enormous operation from Ramstein Air Base (AB) in Germany.

JTF Shining Hope was established on April 4, 1999. The next day forty airmen left for Tirana, the capital of Albania. Their task was to prepare a base camp for the next military units that would work at the airport. The airmen graded roads, erected warehouses in which to store incoming supplies, and set up a dining tent, or mess hall. The crews worked long, hard hours in cold, wet weather. But they knew the refugees in the mountains were living in far worse conditions and were in desperate need of help.

As the Air Force conducted bombing raids against Serbia, the second group of airmen arrived in Tirana, Albania. Their job was to repair the airport's runway and roads in preparation for the cargo planes that would carry relief supplies for the refugees.

General Hinton went to Tirana to check on the preparations. About those working he said, "I can only say how proud I am of the military professionals we have conducting this operation day-to-day. They really

During JTF Shining Hope, the Air Force used C-130 Hercules aircraft to bring in food, medical supplies, bedding, and other necessary materials.

care about this mission and they're going to make sure it gets done."[1]

After the airport was ready, giant Air Force transport planes flew in, carrying power generators, loaders, and other heavy equipment needed to handle incoming goods. Relief supplies from thirty-five countries arrived on C-130s, carrying food, tents, bedding, and medical supplies. Aircraft landed around the clock, as many as three hundred airplanes a day. Supplies were then transferred to trucks and helicopters and delivered to the refugees in Albania and Macedonia.

Shelter remained a critical problem for these displaced people. Air Force personnel built a camp inside Albania for the refugees. Engineers first had to drill for water before they put up tents. The weather turned from hard rain to high winds, but within ten days there was enough shelter to house 2,500 people. Camp

Hope opened on May 12, 1999; a military staff of four hundred managed it. By mid-June some 3,400 refugees lived in the camp.

In early June 1999, President Milosevic signed a peace treaty, and the refugees started to return to Kosovo. The Camp Hope staff members, who had developed a special bond with the Kosovars, helped load the people on the buses. When asked if the effort was worth it, one Air Force technical officer said, "You've just to look at the faces of the people you serve out there. That really brings it home because you know that what you're doing is giving them another chance, another chance for hope."[2]

Almost two months after it began, the Air Force's role in this humanitarian effort ended, and the rest of the JTF Shining Hope operation was turned over to the Marine Corps deputy commander and the United Nations. During its first fifty days, JTF Shining Hope had delivered 3,400 tons of food, equipment, and medical supplies. It was one of the largest relief efforts in Air Force history.

Still, the work of the Air Force was not yet over. Secretary of Defense William Cohen ordered Air Force Red Horse (Rapid Engineer Deployable Heavy Operational Repair Squadron Engineer) Squadrons to upgrade the worn Tirana airport. The civil engineers of these squadrons repaired the airport runway, built a ramp for parking planes, installed a drainage system, and paved roads inside and outside the airport. The Red Horse Squadrons then turned over the airport, in

Red Horse Squadron

The Red Horse (Rapid Engineer Deployable Heavy Operational Repair Squadron Engineer) Squadron is a horse of a different color. It was first organized during the Vietnam War. These civil engineers work as a team to construct facilities quickly before military forces move into an area. The combat-trained Red Horse Squadrons often go into hostile environments and work up to fourteen hours a day. In actual combat a squadron may work around the clock, with no time out for sleeping. In 1999, the squadrons completed projects in Albania and in Central America.

The Air Force has three Red Horse Squadrons in the United States: the 819th, at Malmstrom AFB, Montana; the 820th, at Nellis AFB, Nevada; and the 823rd, at Hurlburt Field, Florida.

better condition than they had found it, to the Albanian government.

It took many Air Force personnel working together to make JTF Shining Hope possible. Professionals who participated ranged from the mechanics who maintained the aircraft to the aircrews that flew the planes. Traffic controllers and communication specialists helped direct aircraft. Some Air Force personnel loaded and guarded the relief supplies, while others set up tents and saw to the refugees' needs in Camp Hope. Engineers built runways, roads, and bridges. Many other U.S. Air Force personnel stationed in Europe and in the United States were involved in this humanitarian mission. Through their efforts they

Airlifting relief supplies is one of the many jobs Air Force personnel handle.

demonstrated the Air Force's core values: "integrity first, service before self, and excellence in all we do."[3]

Finding Out About Air Force Opportunities

The Air Force personnel who participated in Shining Hope represented some of the many career professionals who belong to this military organization. There are over 150 different career fields each for officers and enlisted people in the United States Air Force. Information about these careers can be obtained from local Air Force recruiters or can be found on the Internet.

Two youth organizations, the Air Force Junior Reserve Officer Training Corps (JROTC) and the Civil Air Patrol (CAP) cadet program, offer other ways to learn about the Air Force.

Junior Reserve Officer Training Corps (JROTC)

Located in over six hundred schools in the United States, the Air Force JROTC program is designed to provide citizenship training and an aerospace science program for high school students. Its objectives are "to educate and train high school cadets in citizenship; promote community service; instill responsibility, character, and self-discipline, and provide instruction in air and space fundamentals."[4]

To join an Air Force JROTC program, students must be in the ninth grade or higher, be physically fit, and be citizens of the United States (or citizens of other countries who have been lawfully admitted to this country).

Once they join, students belong to a cadet corps, where they learn military customs and flag etiquette. Cadets participate in drill team competitions, in honor guards, and in color guards. Physical fitness is emphasized in the cadet corps.

Taught by retired Air Force officers, the JROTC curriculum focuses on leadership education and aerospace science. Cadets learn principles of aircraft flight and navigation from textbooks and from hands-on projects, such as constructing model Air Force planes. Some high school JROTC units have access to flight simulators, devices that mimic, or simulate, the sensations and techniques of flying an aircraft. Cadets are also introduced to space programs and space technology. They learn about rocketry and rocket propulsion and may construct and launch small rockets.

In addition to classroom instruction, cadets take field trips to Air Force bases, local airports, aviation museums, and aerospace industries. In some JROTC programs, an Air Force C-130 cargo plane flies in from its home base and airlifts the cadets for short distances.

Citizenship is another important part of the JROTC program. Cadets not only study citizenship, they also put it into practice by doing community work. Collecting canned goods for food drives and cleaning up local parks are typical projects. Cadets also work with national organizations such as the Special

Olympics and the March of Dimes. Students in Air Force JROTC programs help in drug abuse prevention programs by making presentations to elementary and middle school students.

Air Force JROTC cadets who have completed the program enjoy certain advantages. For example, if students want to enlist in the Air Force immediately after high school and they have taken three semesters of JROTC, they may enter the Air Force at two pay grades higher than other enlistees. High school JROTC graduates who enter a college ROTC program take one less year of ROTC instruction.

In the JROTC, cadets take field trips to learn about Air Force opportunities. Here a group of cadets listen as San Antonio Spurs coach Gregg Popovich talks about life in the military.

These students also have the opportunity to compete for Air Force ROTC scholarships.

Civil Air Patrol (CAP) Cadet Program

The Civil Air Patrol (CAP) cadet program is part of a civilian organization that provides advice and assistance to the United States Air Force. Started a few days before the Pearl Harbor bombing, CAP is an official civilian support group, or auxiliary. CAP provides emergency services by maintaining a high-frequency radio network during disasters. Using their own airplanes, CAP members also help in search and rescue missions within the United States. In fact, statistics from Civil Air Patrol headquarters verify that thousands of lives have been saved through CAP search and rescue efforts.[5]

Another CAP mission is providing a cadet program for young people. The CAP cadet program has more than 24,000 members, ages twelve to twenty-one. Like the Air Force JROTC program, the CAP cadet program emphasizes leadership, personal discipline, and patriotism. Cadets receive instruction in aerospace education, develop physical fitness, and work in a leadership laboratory. Moral and ethical leadership is also emphasized.[6]

In aerospace education, cadets learn about principles of flight, navigation, spacecraft and aircraft, weather, and traffic control. CAP students may also attend a CAP program on experimental aircraft.

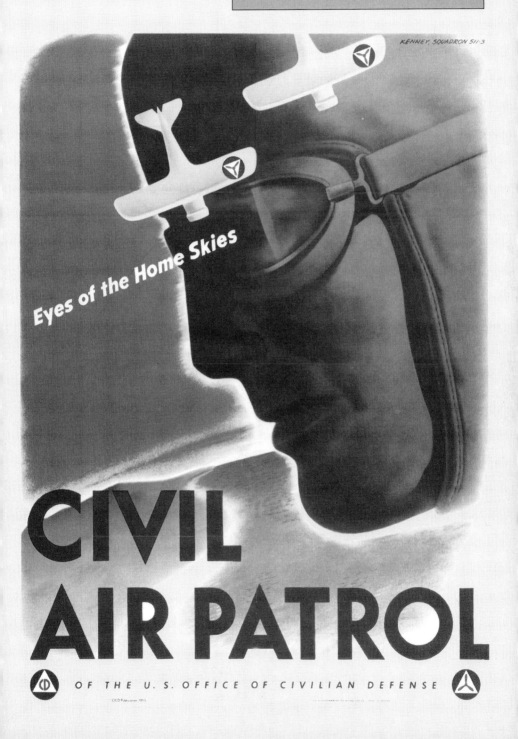

A poster for the Civil Air Patrol from World War II. The patrol is a civilian organization that provides advice and assistance to the U.S. Air Force.

KENNEY, SQUADRON 511-3

Eyes of the Home Skies

CIVIL AIR PATROL

OF THE U. S. OFFICE OF CIVILIAN DEFENSE

In the leadership laboratory, cadets learn and practice leadership and management techniques. The CAP cadet program is based on rank, much like the U.S. Air Force. Students advance through the ranks from cadet basic to cadet colonel, completing certain achievements in each. To increase leadership abilities and advance in rank, students can attend yearly activities such as the Cadet Officer School.

CAP cadets are eligible to participate in summer camps and special activities at Air Force bases. They also have opportunities to receive training in radio communications, aircraft, and gliders. Other programs include a computer orientation program and an orientation course at an Air Force base. Cadets can take rescue courses offered at three U.S. locations during the summer.

Another CAP cadet program open to those who are seventeen or older is the International Air Cadet exchange program. Accompanied by adult CAP members, cadets can visit other cadets in any of the participating eighteen countries. Foreign students can also come to this country for a nineteen-day stay.

The Air Force JROTC and CAP cadets welcome young women and minorities in their programs. Cadets are not obligated to join the Air Force after they participate. By joining the JROTC and the CAP cadet programs, young people learn much about leadership, aerospace, and the world of the United States Air Force.

History of the Air Force

War was first waged from the air in 1851, when Austrian troops in hot-air balloons dropped bombs on Venice, Italy. Balloons were also used in warfare by the United States during the Civil War. The Union lofted men in balloons to survey Confederate troop positions during the battle for Richmond, Virginia. Balloonist Thaddeus Lowe used this information to draw a map of enemy positions and to direct artillery fire on the southern forces. Lowe established the Balloon Service of the Army of the Potomac, which was the first U.S. "air force."[1]

Drawing on his Civil War experience, Brigadier General Aldophus Greely of the Army Signal Corps used balloon surveillance during the Spanish-American War in 1892. Six years later, the Corps gave $50,000 to Samuel Langley, Secretary of the Smithsonian

Institution, to develop a powered heavier-than-air machine. Langley's Aerodrome was launched twice in 1903 and failed both times. On December 17 of that year, less than two weeks after Langley's failure, Wilbur and Orville Wright successfully flew their engine-powered airplane at Kitty Hawk, North Carolina.

But the Army was more interested in a steerable airship, or dirigible. In 1908, the Army ordered its first airship, Dirigible No. 1, costing $6,750. Unfortunately, it crashed, killing Signal Corps Lieutenant Thomas Selfridge, a passenger, and injuring Orville Wright, who was at the controls. Lieutenant Selfridge, a pilot himself, had been the first

soldier to fly a heavier-than-air machine on May 19, 1908. He was the first military aviation casualty.

In 1909, the Army paid the Wright brothers $30,000 for developing an improved version of their plane; the new model was named Airplane No. 1. They received an additional $5,000 because the plane exceeded the speed requirement of 40 miles per hour. Wilbur Wright taught three men, Lieutenants Benjamin D. Foulois, Frederick E. Humphreys, and Frank P. Lahm, how to fly the plane. Each of the men actually soloed in Airplane No. 1. They became the first pilots to fly the world's first military airplane.

Pleased with the plane's success, Congress gave the Army money in 1911 for more aircraft. However, the airplanes were flying deathtraps. Between 1909 and 1913 there were twenty-four qualified army aviators. Eleven were killed while still in training and seven more died in subsequent crashes.[2]

It was not until March 1916 that airplanes were put into combat. President Woodrow Wilson ordered General John Pershing to capture the

Balloons were first used in warfare by the United States during the Civil War. Union forces used the balloons to see where the Confederate troops were located. In the picture, troops are getting a balloon ready for liftoff.

Mexican revolutionary and bandit Pancho Villa. Villa had killed eight American citizens in Mexico; then he crossed over the border into New Mexico, where he killed a total of sixteen soldiers and citizens. Pershing's forces included the 1st Aero Squadron—ten pilots, eight aircraft, ten trucks, one automobile, and six motorcycles.

The 1st Aero Squadron did not do well. The pilots had limited flying experience, since flying was just in its infancy, and the wooden, fabric-covered trainer aircraft, JN-3 "Jennies," were not very sturdy. Also, these trainer airplanes were not able to fly over mountains that were higher than a thousand feet, and the Jennies were affected by the harsh desert conditions. Even so, the 1st Aero Squadron was successful at finding lost cavalry and carrying mail. But the squadron's true significance probably is the fact that between March and August 1916, these novice pilots flew 540 missions and maintained communication with Pershing's troops, which had penetrated 700 miles into Mexico.

World War I

In August 1914, World War I began in Europe, with Russia, Britain, and France (known as the Allies) fighting against Germany, Austria, and Italy. When the United States entered the war in April 1917, it had only fifty-six pilots and fewer than 250 old airplanes. Except for a few shops that built aircraft by hand, this country had no aircraft industry or workers. In spite of

When General John Pershing went into Mexico, his forces included the 1st Aero Squadron. This squadron flew 540 missions and kept in communication with Pershing's troops, which had penetrated 700 miles into Mexico.

this, there was talk of "darkening the skies over Germany with clouds of U.S. aircraft."[3]

President Wilson ordered all-out airplane production. Spruce forests were downed, and most of the lumber was shipped to Britain and France for aircraft production. The United States built about fourteen thousand airplanes, half of which were Jennies. The United States also made and shipped aircraft engines to its allies.

American airmen were not put into the skies until almost the end of the war. Pilots flew reconnaissance missions over France, where they observed enemy troop movement and reported their findings back to headquarters. Airmen flew cover for Allied troops and dropped artillery on German soldiers. Allied pilots fought savage aerial dogfights with enemy pilots, in which each pilot attempted to shoot the other down.

Airmen also flew patrols in order to find isolated ground troops. Two airmen, Lieutenant Harold Goettler and Second Lieutenant Erwin Bleckley, of the 50th Aero Squadron, were flying low, looking for a "Lost Battalion," when they were shot down and killed. After they died, the United States awarded the two pilots Medals of Honor, the nation's highest award for extraordinary bravery during combat.

The greatest aerial battle during the war occurred September 12–15, 1918, over Saint-Mihiel, France. The Allies planned an attack on a German line that extended twenty-four miles across and fourteen miles deep at its biggest point. Brigadier General William

"Billy" Mitchell commanded nearly fifteen hundred American aircraft. For more than two weeks before the battle, U.S. and French pilots photographed German troop positions and movements.

When the battle began, Allied bombers flew ahead of advancing troops and strafed enemy lines. Pursuit, or fighter, pilots engaged in fierce air battles with German airmen. By the time the battle ended, pilots had made 3,300 flights, fired 30,000 rounds of ammunition, dropped 75 tons of explosives, and destroyed more than 60 German aircraft.[4] Two American pilots, Second Lieutenant Frank Luke and

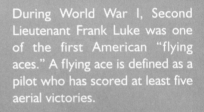

During World War I, Second Lieutenant Frank Luke was one of the first American "flying aces." A flying ace is defined as a pilot who has scored at least five aerial victories.

Captain Eddie Rickenbacker, became the first American "flying aces." (An ace is a pilot who has scored at least five aerial victories.) Both earned Medals of Honor, though Luke's medal was awarded posthumously (after his death).

World War I ended on November 11, 1918. This "war to end all wars" left a total of ten million people dead from all participating countries. Pilots suffered casualty rates of 50 percent or more in some squadrons. The air force had entered the combat age. World War I convinced General Mitchell of the need for air power, and he argued for a separate air force. He was court-martialed (tried in a military court) for publicly criticizing his Army superiors, though he was later acquitted, or found not guilty. Many of his predictions about the role of air power in war came true during the next war.

Between the World Wars

After World War I, the Army cut back its airplane orders. Advances in aviation technology continued, however. New designs made planes fly faster, farther, and higher. Metal was substituted for wood. Airplane instruments were developed, which told the pilot the plane's speed, altitude, and location. This enabled pilots to fly at night or in cloudy skies.

Airplanes were also used for civilian (nonmilitary) purposes. Aircraft dropped relief supplies to communities suffering from natural disasters. The newly named Army Air Corps delivered the U.S. mail.

Captain Edward "Eddie" Rickenbacker
(1890–1973)
World War I Flying Ace

Starting as an enlisted driver, Eddie Rickenbacker became a pilot during World War I. On his first combat mission over France, he shot down two German planes. The following month he downed eleven enemy planes and three balloons. In less than six months, he had twenty-six victories and was awarded the Medal of Honor.

During World War II, while he was on a mission as a civilian troubleshooter, Rickenbacker's plane was shot down and crash-landed at sea. He and seven airmen drifted in life rafts for twenty-four days. Under Captain Edward Rickenbacker's leadership, all but one man survived.

Barnstormers—traveling pilots who gave plane rides to sightseers and performed daredevil stunts for an audience—crisscrossed the country. Many of them were former war pilots. For many Americans, barnstormers provided their first look at this wondrous invention. Unfortunately, because of the number of crashes and high fatality rate of these pilots, aviation was perceived as something for crazy people. Eventually, the U.S. government put major restrictions on barnstormers. Then, with solo flights across the Atlantic Ocean by Charles Lindbergh in 1927 and by Amelia Earhart five years later, the American public began to accept the idea of aviation and the possibilities it could offer.

During the 1930s, Germany, led by Adolf Hitler, began to threaten its European neighbors once again. United States

General Henry "Hap" Arnold
(1886–1950)
Five-Star General of the Air Force

Henry H. Arnold was taught to fly by the Wright brothers. When he graduated from West Point in 1907, Arnold wanted a cavalry command. Put in the infantry, he later joined the Army Signal Corps and became one of the first military pilots. He rose in rank—constantly pushing his Army superiors for an air force—to become commanding general of the Army Air Forces during World War II. He later became the Air Force's first, and only, five-star general.

Nicknamed "Hap" (for "happy," because of his constant smile), Arnold was impatient, blunt, and brilliant. Because of his vision and drive, the United States became a great air power.

president Franklin D. Roosevelt ordered greater aircraft production. Still, when Germany invaded Poland in September 1939, the United States was poorly equipped for war.

General Henry H. "Hap" Arnold, chief of the Army Air Corps, established flight schools to train military pilots. General Arnold urged companies to produce more military planes, which they did. However, Congress initially held back money, because of antiwar sentiment. The fear prevailed that increased production would draw the United States into the war. Actually, the United States lent many of its new planes to its allies: Great Britain, France, and the Soviet Union.

World War II

On December 7, 1941, Japan attacked the American fleet at Pearl Harbor, Hawaii. President Roosevelt called it "a date which will live in infamy." The United States declared war on Japan the following day and on its allies, Germany and Italy, a few days later. The United States had entered World War II. General Hap Arnold was made commander of the Army Air Forces.

The entire country threw its mighty collective energy into waging this second global war. Men were drafted or enlisted, and women volunteered for military duty. Aircraft factories ran around the clock. Women left their housework to work alongside men on the assembly lines and earned for themselves the nickname "Rosie the Riveter." Auxiliary groups such as the Women's Army Auxiliary Corps (WAAC) assisted the Army Air Forces. Minority pilots, such as the Tuskegee Airmen under the command of Lieutenant General Benjamin Davis, Jr., also participated in the war effort.

Two-engine bombers such as B-25s and B-26s proved effective against Japanese forces in the Pacific. Pilots in four-engine bombers, B-17s and B-24s, dropped bombs on German and Italian forces. B-29s struck Japan. Fighter planes escorted big bombers and engaged in aerial dogfights to protect the bombers. The fighters also strafed enemy positions and destroyed or disrupted supply and transportation lines.

Large cargo planes, C-46s and C-47s, were essential for transporting troops and supplies. Some pilots were assigned the job of delivering supplies to Allied forces in China. Lifting off from bases in India, the airmen had to fly over the Himalayas, "the Hump," as they called the mountain range. They flew through 19,000-foot mountain passes in the most brutal weather conditions.

On June 6, 1944, better known as D day, the Allies, under the command of General Dwight D. Eisenhower, launched "Operation Overlord," a massive assault against German forces in Europe. Historian Stephen Ambrose describes the giant air armada as it approached the French coast: "It took 432 C-47s to carry the 101st Airborne . . . , about the same number for the 82nd. They were flying in a V-of-Vs

A B-25 takes off from the USS *Hornet* on its way to take part in air raids on Japan. The United States effectively used combat aircraft against Japanese forces in the Pacific.

formation, stretched out across the sky, 300 miles long, nine planes wide, without radio communication."[5]

The planes dropped paratroopers behind enemy lines, allowing them to capture key bridges and flank the enemy. Many paratroopers were killed. Despite great loss of life, the assault was successful and the Allies pressed on through Europe.

Germany finally surrendered on May 8, 1945. Japan continued fighting until Air Force B-29s dropped atomic bombs on the Japanese cities of Hiroshima and Nagasaki. Officially, World War II ended on August 14, 1945. During this global war, out of the 2,244,000 Army Air Force personnel who served, 52,153 were killed. As General William "Billy"

Paratroopers being dropped into Holland, September, 1944.

Mitchell had predicted, air power had determined the outcome of the war.

After World War II

In 1947, the Air Force became a separate branch of the United States armed forces. General Carl A. Spaatz, hero in two wars, was appointed chief of staff of the United States Air Force.

The Air Force advanced with new aircraft technology. First developed during World War II, jet-powered engines were further refined. Pilots tested experimental planes that flew more than 600 miles per hour.

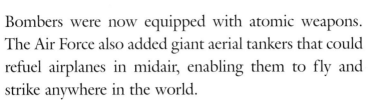

Bombers were now equipped with atomic weapons. The Air Force also added giant aerial tankers that could refuel airplanes in midair, enabling them to fly and strike anywhere in the world.

After the Allies defeated Germany in World War II, they divided the country into East Germany, which was Communist, and West Germany, which was not. The city of Berlin was also divided, with East Berlin controlled by the Soviet Union and West Berlin controlled by the United States and Great Britain. Hoping that the Allies would abandon West Berlin, in June 1948 the Soviet Union threw a blockade around the western part of the city so that people and supplies could not pass through.

In "Operation Vittles," the United States airlifted food and fuel to two million Berliners for more than a year.[6] Cargo planes flew in and out around the clock. Toward the end of the year, they were landing every

Sergeant Henry E. "Red" Erwin
World War II Hero

In April 1944, Sergeant Erwin was flying on a B-29 attack mission over Japan. His job was dropping phosphorous bombs. As he dropped one bomb, it flew back into his face, blinding him and burning off one ear. Smoke filled the cockpit. Knowing the 1,300-degree bomb would burn through the plane floor, he tossed it out the copilot's window.

The plane made an emergency landing at Iwo Jima. While medics worked to save Erwin, officials rushed through the Medal of Honor so that he could have it before he died.

Sergeant Red Erwin survived and worked as a benefits counselor at a veteran's hospital for thirty-seven years.

30.9 seconds. Eight thousand tons of food and coal were delivered daily. By the time the blockade ended, more than two million tons of supplies had been delivered. This great humanitarian effort was known as the Berlin Airlift.

In 1950, the Soviet Union exploded its first atomic bomb, five years after the United States first tested its atomic bomb. An arms race began in which the two countries competed to see which could develop the most atomic weapons. Named the Cold War, it was a period during which the two countries were not directly engaged in fighting but kept each other in

During "Operation Vittles," C-47 cargo planes like these airlifted food and fuel to Berliners for over a year.

check with production of nuclear weapons and the threat of nuclear war.

In March 1946, the Air Force created the Strategic Air Command (SAC), led by General Curtis LeMay. SAC emphasized the importance of strategic, or long-range, bomber forces in the Air Force. U.S. leaders believed that the development of strategic nuclear weapons would prevent war because it would deter other countries from attacking the United States.

The Korean War

In 1950, trouble developed in Asia when North Korea invaded South Korea. The United Nations asked its members to come to the defense of South Korea. North Korea had the support of the Soviet Union, which provided military supplies, and of China, which provided supplies and troops.

In the Korean War, the United States launched bombing strikes to stop the flow of materials and men into South Korea. Initially, the outdated U.S. propeller-plane fighters were no match for the Soviet-built fighter aircraft used by the North Koreans. Finally, the Air Force sent its new jet fighters, the F-80 Shooting Star and the F-86 Sabre, into action. The F-86 Sabre was superior to the Soviet-built M-15, the mainstay fighter of the North Koreans.

U.S. pilots were forbidden to penetrate the airspace of the Soviet Union and China because the United Nations did not want these countries drawn into another major war. Peace talks started in 1951,

During the Korean War, the newly formed U.S. Air Force used the highly advanced F-86 Sabre to fight the North Koreans. These F-86 airplanes are on the flight line getting ready for battle.

but the fighting continued. By the time the Korean War ended in July 1953, twenty different governments on six continents had participated.[7] Fifty-four thousand Americans died in this war.

After the war ended, the Soviet Union and the United States continued to compete to see which nation could develop more sophisticated weapons. The United States also developed unmanned missiles that carried nuclear warheads. These missiles could be launched from the ground or carried by planes.

In 1957, the Soviet Union launched the first man-made satellite, called *Sputnik*. The United States then accelerated its own space program. The two countries

Brigadier General Charles "Chuck" E. Yeager
(1923–)
Fighter Pilot, Test Pilot

Starting as a World War II plane mechanic, Chuck Yeager became a much-decorated fighter pilot. During one mission, he downed a record number of five German planes. He was shot down over France, and, although wounded, he carried a fellow pilot over rugged mountains to safety. He also flew combat missions during the Korean War and the war in Vietnam.

Yeager is best known as a test pilot. In October 1947, flying with broken ribs, he became the first person to break the sound barrier. He flew a Bell X-1, *Glamorous Glennis*, named for his wife. His plane now hangs at the Smithsonian's National Air and Space Museum.

In 1957, the Soviet Union launched the first man-made satellite, called *Sputnik*, into space. After the launch, the United States stepped up its own space program.

raced to see which one would dominate space. By the 1960s, the United States had become a force in space.

The Air Force launched a satellite system that circled the earth, gathering information with its sophisticated instruments. These satellites could detect enemy missiles that might be fired toward the United States. The Air Force also developed a system of satellites that could monitor weather conditions around the globe.

The Vietnam War

Trouble had been building in the country of Vietnam in Southeast Asia for many years. Formerly a French colony, in 1954 Vietnam was divided into two countries, North Vietnam and South Vietnam. The government of North Vietnam was Communist and was backed by China and the Soviet Union, while the non-Communist government of South Vietnam was backed by the United States. The North Vietnamese government provided arms and training to people in South Vietnam, known as the Vietcong, who opposed their government.

In 1961, U.S. President John Kennedy sent military advisors to help the South Vietnamese government. The following year, 10,000 U.S. troops were sent to South Vietnam. The Vietcong continued to fight. They occupied most of South Vietnam, and the United States became committed to stopping them.

In 1962, the Air Force launched the controversial Operation Ranch Hand, which dropped herbicides to

Lieutenant Edwin E. "Buzz" Aldrin, Jr.
(1930–)
Fighter Pilot, Astronaut

Buzz Aldrin was the second man to set foot on the moon. He and Neil Armstrong landed on the lunar surface on July 20, 1969. Aldrin also piloted the 1966 *Gemini 12* space flight, in which he "walked" in space for five and a half hours.

Aldrin graduated from West Point (the Army's military academy) in 1961 but entered the Air Force for pilot training. He flew sixty-two combat missions in Korea. He earned his Ph.D. from Massachusetts Institute of Technology and became an astronaut in 1963. After leaving the space program, Aldrin commanded the Air Force Test Pilot School.

remove the jungle cover of the Vietcong. On February 2, 1962, a C-123 Ranch Hand aircraft crashed while spraying defoliant herbicides and became the first United States Air Force aircraft lost in South Vietnam. The Air Force conducted a sustained bombing program against the enemy, including three major air campaigns. Operation Rolling Thunder, which started in February 1965 and lasted until March 1968, launched attacks in an effort to stop the flow of men and supplies into South Vietnam and to bring the North Vietnamese to peace talks.

In 1972, President Richard Nixon authorized the second major bombing attack, called Operation Linebacker I. Linebacker II followed, also in 1972. A cease-fire agreement was reached in January of 1973, and U.S. troops were withdrawn. In 1975, South Vietnam surrendered to North Vietnam.

The Vietnam War was unpopular in the United States, resulting in a loss of support to wage the war. It also resulted in President Johnson's decision not to seek another term of office.

During the 1970s, the United States and the Soviet Union signed treaties to end their competitive stock-piling of nuclear weapons. In the late 1980s, the former Soviet Union held its first relatively free elections and formed a new government. Finally, in 1990, the giant wall that separated East Berlin and West Berlin was knocked down, and the country of Germany was united once again. The Cold War had ended.

The Flying Aces

An ace is defined as a pilot who has scored at least five aerial victories.

Leading wartime aces and their scores:

World War I
Captain Eddie Rickenbacker, 26

World War II
Major Richard Bong, 40

Korean War
Captain Joseph McConnell, Jr., 16

Vietnam War
Captain Charles DeBellevue, 6

Leading aces of two different wars and their scores:

Colonel Francis "Gabby" Gabreski (34½*)
World War II: 28
Korean War: 6½*

Colonel John C. Meyer (26)
World War II: 24
Korean War: 2

* Shared credit with another aviator.

Persian Gulf War

The Air Force continued to develop new planes and new technology in keeping with the theory that the latest technology and preparedness for war act as a deterrent to the next war. Nevertheless, war came to the Middle East in 1990. The country of Iraq invaded the tiny oil-rich country of Kuwait, which borders the Persian Gulf. Fearing this nearby threat, Saudi Arabia asked for protection. The United States acted to defend the area with the help of more than twenty other member countries of the United Nations, including Egypt, France, and Great Britain.

The allies had two operations. First was Operation Desert Shield, a six-month buildup of weapons and personnel, which developed air, ground, and naval forces to defend Saudi

Arabia and its vast oil reserves. Second was Operation Desert Storm, which used those forces to attack Iraqi forces in Kuwait and inside the borders of Iraq itself.

The air offensive began in January 1991 with night attacks on Iraqi radar sites, missiles, and communication centers. By this time the Air Force had already developed stealth bombers and fighters as well as the Patriot missile system and laser-guided bombs. The new stealth F-117 fighters, which were extremely difficult to detect by radar, struck at the downtown area of Baghdad, the Iraqi capital. Satellite communications enabled millions of people to watch this attack on television.

Following heavy losses to American Air Force fighters, Saddam Hussein's aircraft fled into neighboring Iran. The United States and its allies used

During Operation Desert Storm, the Air Force used the new stealth F-117 fighters. These aircraft were extremely difficult to detect on radar and were the primary aircraft used for strikes against the Iraqi capital of Baghdad.

Stealth Planes

Stealth planes are aircraft that are difficult to detect by radar. This is made possible by giving the planes special aerodynamic shapes and making the surfaces out of carbon-graphite composites. This black material absorbs radar waves or bounces them away from the sender. The engines on stealth aircraft are designed to conceal the plane's heated exhaust, which makes the aircraft susceptible to detection.

The Air Force presently has two types of stealth aircraft: bombers and fighters. The B-1B and the newer B-2 (pictured below), which were first used in 1999 during the war in Bosnia, are both bombers. The F-117 fighter was first sent on a special operation in Panama in 1989 and saw action during the Persian Gulf War in 1991.

information from satellites about troop movements and targets inside Iraq. Stealth fighters and bombers struck at the Iraqi soldiers from high altitudes. Iraq launched missiles against the allied forces. One landed in Saudi Arabia, killing 28 Americans.

The final military offensive, under the command of General H. Norman Schwarzkopf, came in February 1991 when the allied forces launched the ground war. Air forces cut off the enemy's retreat into Iraq and continued bombing inside the country. Within three days, the allies controlled the capital of Kuwait and the Iraqis surrendered.

The new stealth technology and information-gathering satellites were vital in helping the allies defeat the Iraqis. But the Persian Gulf War could not have been won without the cooperation and the great coordination between the combined U.S. armed forces and the other allies.

Joining the Air Force

How do you join the Air Force? It depends on whether you want to enter the Air Force as an enlisted person or as an officer. It also depends on whether you want to serve full-time on active duty or serve part-time in the Reserve or Air National Guard. An Air Force recruiter, listed in the local telephone directory, has the latest information on the requirements, training, and career opportunities of each.

Enlisted Personnel

It is possible to enlist in the Air Force immediately after high school. You have to be a high school graduate and be between ages of seventeen and twenty-seven (if you are seventeen, you need parental permission to enlist). The Air Force also requires those who join to be physically fit and drug-free, with no criminal record.

A candidate must pass the Armed Services Vocational Aptitude Battery, a series of tests that examine language, math, general science, mechanics, and problem-solving skills. The results of these tests enable the Air Force to determine what skills a person has.

If someone is interested in joining the Air Force, they can go see an Air Force recruiter. A recruiter has the latest information on requirements, training, and career opportunities.

Next the applicant goes to one of the Military Entrance Processing Stations located in large cities across the country. Here the applicant presents his or her birth certificate, social security card, driver's license, high school records, and doctor's records. The recruit takes a physical, which includes an eye test and a dental check. Every recruit is tested for drug use and diseases.

Applicants are then fingerprinted and interviewed by an Air Force counselor, who uses a computer to match the career the person is interested in with the careers and skills the Air Force needs at that time. The applicant then signs a binding contract, making at least a four-year commitment to the Air Force, and takes an oath of enlistment.

Every enlistee goes to Lackland Air Force Base (AFB) in San Antonio, Texas, for basic military training (BMT). Home of the 737th Training Group, Lackland trains about 35,000 new recruits a year.

BMT lasts six weeks and includes physical training, field training, drill, and classroom instruction. Women and men go through the same training.

Each recruit is assigned to a "flight," consisting of thirty to sixty people. The flights have military instructors who are responsible for basic training. Recruits stay with their flight group and military instructors for the entire six weeks.

During the first week, recruits get haircuts, uniforms, and equipment and are assigned to a dorm room. The training day starts at 5:00 A.M. and ends with the playing of "Taps" and lights out at

During the first week of basic military training, recruits get haircuts, uniforms, and equipment. These recruits from Flights 569 and 570 get their first military haircuts, as fellow recruits wait for their turn.

9:00 P.M. Trainees are served three meals a day. Each day, time is scheduled for personal hygiene, dorm maintenance, physical conditioning (PC), and study time, as well as training.

Physical conditioning is scheduled at least six times a week. A trainee's physical condition is evaluated the first weekend after arrival and about midway through training. These evaluations include a timed two-mile run, push-ups, and sit-ups. All trainees have to pass the PC test to graduate. An obstacle course with twenty-one stations is designed to test a trainee's physical and mental abilities. It also builds confidence and develops flight teamwork.

Trainees take field training to learn basic survival skills. Everyone spends a day and a half at a site about five miles from the base. During field

Obstacle courses challenge the recruits' physical and mental abilities.

Salute

The salute is a required military greeting, intended to show courtesy and respect. Salutes are required at various time between members of the military, when the national anthem is played, at military funerals, when the flag is honored, and at other official ceremonies.

Saluting evolved in the Middle Ages, when a knight raised the face visor on his helmet as a greeting. By doing so, the knight had to remove his hand from his sword, which made him vulnerable. The gesture showed friendship and confidence.

training, the instructors act as the enemy and attack the camp, which the trainees defend. Field training is structured to resemble combat conditions as much as possible.

The last week before graduation, trainees participate in Warrior Week. For seven days, trainees live in a 1,000-tent city outside camp, where they are exposed to combatlike conditions. The purpose of the exercise is to create readiness to fight in the case of actual war. After successfully completing Warrior Week, the trainees are called "airmen," a term that applies to both men and women. Airmen graduate the last week, with family members invited to attend.

After graduation, airmen report to one of the Air Force's technical training schools. Training is usually conducted at one of four main bases: Keesler AFB in Mississippi, or Sheppard AFB, Goodfellow AFB, or Lackland AFB in Texas. Technical training periods last from four to fifty-two weeks, depending on the specialty. After training, each airman is assigned to an Air Force base for duty.[1]

Enlisted Pay and Benefits

Active-duty enlisted personnel are paid a basic salary every month. Pay is tied to years of service and grade, or rank. Grades are listed according to rank from Airman Basic, E-1, through Chief Master Sergeant, E-9, the highest enlisted rank in the Air Force. The higher the rank and years of service, the higher the base pay.

In addition to base pay, the Air Force gives bonuses to those who enlist in certain needed Air Force careers, such as air-traffic control. If an enlistee volunteers to work in a hazardous occupation, such as handling toxic materials, that person is paid extra. Bonuses are also paid for reenlisting in the Air Force. A clothing allowance (for uniforms) is given yearly to every airman. A cost-of-living raise is given every year.

Other benefits include free medical and dental care and thirty days of vacation with pay each year. The Air Force also provides free living quarters on base for

A member of the Strategic Air Command Disaster Response Force checks an aircraft for possible radiation exposure. The Air Force pays extra to enlistees who volunteer to work in hazardous occupations.

single airmen. Enlisted personnel with families are given on-base housing or a monthly allowance for housing off base. Dining facilities on base are available with no or low-cost meals. Recreational facilities and low-cost shopping are also available on Air Force bases.

The Air Force offers excellent educational benefits. Through Community College of the Air Force (CCAF), airmen can receive college credit for their technical training and obtain an associate degree. They can also take courses at accredited colleges and universities on off-duty time, with 75 percent of tuition paid. In addition, the Air Force has the Extension Course Institute, a free correspondence school offering about

Air Force Enlisted Personnel Ranks and Pay Grades

Pay Grade	Rank
E-9	Chief Master Sergeant of the Air Force
E-9	Command Chief Master Sergeant
E-9	Chief Master Sergeant
E-8	Senior Master Sergeant
E-7	Master Sergeant
E-6	Technical Sergeant
E-5	Staff Sergeant
E-4	Senior Airman
E-3	Airman First Class
E-2	Airman
E-1	Airman Basic

four hundred courses. Retirement benefits are available after twenty years of service.

Officers

Air Force pilots, navigators, and unit commanders are just a few of the professions that require commissioned officers. To qualify as an officer, one has to be eighteen through thirty years of age, have graduated from a four-year college, be a United States citizen, and have excellent moral character.

The U.S. Air Force offers several officer training programs. The two largest programs, the Air Force Reserve Officer Training Corps (ROTC) and the Air Force Academy (AFA), start when a person enters college. In return for financial assistance for college, students sign up for four to ten years (depending on the specialty) of Air Force service after graduation.

Air Force ROTC

The largest officer training program is Air Force ROTC, which produces over two thousand new officers a year. One hundred and forty-three Air Force ROTC units exist at colleges and universities in this country and Puerto Rico. The main mission of the Air Force ROTC is "to produce leaders for the Air Force and build better citizens for America."[2]

To be eligible for the Air Force ROTC program, students must be of high moral character and must pass a physical fitness test and a physical examination. Students must also pass a background security check and the Air Force Officer Qualifying Test. Other traits the ROTC commanding officer looks for in an applicant are:

- Positive attitude

- Desire to serve one's country

- Potential for leadership

Once accepted into the Air Force ROTC, students are called "cadets." Those in the ROTC program form a cadet corps.

Air Force ROTC offers two- and four-year programs. The two-year program is primarily for students majoring in special professions such as law or nursing. These students enter Air Force ROTC during the last two years of college. In the four-year program, cadets receive general military instruction courses during their freshman and sophomore years. These are in addition to regular college courses. They have one hour of military coursework once a week, for which they receive college credit. Classes, taught by military officers with at least a master's degree, focus on Air Force structure, history, and military procedure. All ROTC students have to keep at least a 2.0 grade point average (a C average), or higher, depending on the college's minimum requirements. Cadets must also be physically fit and maintain good conduct.

In addition to military coursework, Air Force ROTC cadets take a two-hour laboratory leadership class once a week. In the leadership classes, students learn military customs, practice teamwork, and participate in drill and leadership exercises.

At the end of the sophomore year, cadets attend a four-week leadership camp, or field training, that is held on an Air Force base. Cadets receive training in professional development, physical fitness, marksmanship, and survival skills. Trainees also are given twenty-five to thirty group leadership situations to resolve. The Air Force pays for uniforms, meals, lodging, and travel expenses. Cadets are also paid for the four-week period. Students who enter the two-year

At the end of the sophomore year, ROTC cadets attend field training on an Air Force base. The training includes exercises such as this obstacle course.

Air Force ROTC program must take five weeks of field training.

In order to continue in the four-year ROTC program, cadets have to pass an evaluation by a board and complete field training before the beginning of their junior year. Selection is based on grade point average, scores on the Officer Qualifying Test, physical fitness, the commander's evaluation, and the Air Force physical examination.

Cadets compete for available slots. All junior-level cadets who pass sign a contract with the Air Force and become members of the Air Force Reserve. They are paid a monthly stipend, or allowance, for the last two years of college. Some money is also given for college tuition. The amounts paid are available from the nearest Air Force ROTC office.

During the last two years of college, Air Force ROTC cadets start the professional officer course. In addition to taking two hours of weekly military coursework per week, cadets undergo intensive leadership training. They participate in and conduct the leadership labs; they also direct the cadet corps.

At the end of their senior year, cadets receive commissions as officers in the Air Force. These commissions are given in a separate ceremony at the college. After taking an oath, newly commissioned officers receive their gold-bar insignia, showing that they are now second lieutenants in the U.S. Air Force. They also receive an appointment certificate from the president of the United States, who is also commander in chief of the nation's armed forces. Cadets make at least a four-year commitment to the Air Force.

The Air Force Academy

The Air Force Academy (AFA), near Colorado Springs, Colorado, also produces officers. The Air Force Academy is a competitive, highly selective, and demanding college and officer training school. Only about one in 90–100 applicants is selected. Most of its graduates become pilots or navigators.

To get into the Air Force Academy, a student has to start preparing while a freshman in high school. The student must take a rigorous academic program, including four years of math, science, and English courses. High SAT scores and grade point averages

Graduates of the U.S. Air Force Academy class of 2001 celebrate their achievement.

are required. Students should also have strong backgrounds in athletics and extracurricular activities.

To enter the Air Force Academy, candidates must be at least seventeen years old but not have passed their twenty-third birthday on July 1 of the year entering the Academy. Candidates must be unmarried with no children and must possess high moral character.

The application process begins during the junior year of high school. The candidate should contact a local AFA Admission Liaison Officer for a precandidate questionnaire. (Your high school guidance counselor can provide information on how to reach a Liaison Officer.) After completing the questionnaire, the candidate should take the SAT (Scholastic Assessment Test) or the ACT (American College Test).

An eligible candidate usually needs a nomination from his or her U.S. senator or representative. The candidate makes application to the Academy, attends an interview with the Liaison Officer, and submits a writing sample. Finally, the candidate must pass a medical exam and an AFA candidate fitness test. Deadlines exist for each step of the application process.

Upon entering the Air Force Academy, one becomes a fourth-class cadet, or freshman. The cadet receives a tuition-free education, a monthly allowance, and a daily subsistence for meals. The cadet must bring $2,500 for initial expenses. Every cadet lives in a dorm with a roommate and is provided with a personal computer.

Military instruction begins with the fourth-class cadet taking basic cadet training (BCT), which includes military orientation, drill, daily exercise, and participation in a field training camp. On completing BCT, the cadet becomes a member of the Cadet Wing, the student body.

Cadets continue military instruction during their four years of college. The courses include military history, doctrine, strategy, and leadership. Cadets also take courses in ethics.

Central to ethics is the honor code, which cadets must swear to and abide by. The honor code states, "We will not lie, steal or cheat nor tolerate among us anyone who does."[3]

At the Academy, physical conditioning is emphasized with physical education courses. Extensive athletics include intercollegiate and intramural men's and women's teams. All the twenty-seven varsity

The Air Force Academy Falcons and Falconers

The falcon was chosen as the Air Force Academy mascot by the 1959 graduating class. The bird was picked because of its alertness, keen eyesight, courage, graceful flight, and speed.

The AFA has sixteen falcons, representing all the North American species: kestrel, merlin, prairie, peregrine, and gyrfalcon. It takes six weeks or approximately three hundred man-hours to properly train an eyas, or young falcon. The official AFA mascot is Aurora, a rare female white phase arctic gyrfalcon.

The AFA falconers consist of twelve cadets, four students each from the sophomore, junior, and senior classes. To be selected, a cadet must learn about falcons, pass a written state exam, and be chosen by the falconry team.

Supervised by a veterinarian officer, falconers care for the birds every day, year-round. They weigh and feed the birds to maintain an ideal weight (an overweight bird does not want to fly; a lightweight one can be damaged during flight). The cadets fly the falcons for two hours a day, except during molting season. Senior falconers name the birds—a great honor!

sports teams are called the Falcons, named after the Air Force Academy mascot.

The Academy has high academic standards. The first two years, cadets take the required core curriculum, which includes English, history, biology, math, physics, foreign languages, and aeronautical and astronautical engineering. At the junior level, each cadet selects one from among the thirty-one major courses of study available.

Third-class cadets (those in their sophomore year) can participate in the Academy's Soaring Program. Twenty-one courses are offered in gliding, piloting, and parachuting. After this basic flight training, cadets progress to flying highly sophisticated planes. Flight safety is emphasized in all the flying courses.

After four years of study, cadets graduate with a bachelor of science degree and an officer's commission. They must make at least a five-year basic commitment to serve in the U.S. Air Force. Pilots make a ten-year total commitment, while navigators must serve six years.

Other Officer Training Programs

In addition to Air Force ROTC and the Air Force Academy, there are several other ways to become an officer. The Air Force has a twelve-week Officer Training School (OTS) for those who are already college graduates and a four-week program for those with further professional training who wish to become

Captain Katarina S. Bentler, pilot of a KC-135 Stratotanker, confers with her copilot. Pilots make a ten-year commitment to serve in the Air Force.

USAF Thunderbirds

The Air Force's precision-flying squadron is called the Thunderbirds. The squadron consists of twelve F-16 fighter planes, six of which are used in performance. There are eight pilots (including six demonstration pilots), four support officers, and approximately 104 enlisted personnel in the squadron. The Thunderbirds perform intricate aerial maneuvers in a variety of formations. Teamwork and communication are vital for successful precision formations.

Those flying are experienced fighter pilots who serve two-year assignments. They train from November to March, giving about sixty performances the remainder of the year. The demonstrations last for over an hour.

Originally called Stardusters, the squadron's name was changed to Thunderbirds because of the bird's exalted place in Native American mythology.

medical service officers, judge advocates (military lawyers), or chaplains (military clergy).

Officer Pay and Benefits

Officers receive basic pay, which varies according to grade (based on rank) and years of service. Pay grades range from O-1 for second lieutenant to O-10, the rank of commanding general. The higher the rank and the greater the number of years served, the higher the pay.

In addition to basic pay, the Air Force gives certain officers extra pay. For example, those who have certain

Air Force Officer Ranks and Pay Grades

Pay Grade	Rank
O-10	General
O-9	Lieutenant General
O-8	Major General
O-7	Brigadier General
O-6	Colonel
O-5	Lieutenant Colonel
O-4	Major
O-3	Captain
O-2	First Lieutenant
O-1	Second Lieutenant

The Hurricane Hunters

Reservists from the 53rd Weather Reconnaissance Squadron stationed at Keesler AFB in Mississippi track hurricanes and tropical storms threatening the Atlantic coastline and the Gulf of Mexico. In specially equipped WC-130s, the pilots fly into the eyes of storms to gather weather information.

During a mission, the crew flies into the storm center four times. Each time, an operator fires an eighteen-inch cardboard cylinder containing sensitive equipment. As the cylinder descends in a parachute, it transmits data on wind speed and direction, barometric pressure, temperature, and humidity. This information is sent by satellite to the National Hurricane Center in Miami, Florida.

needed skills (such as dental or medical officers) and those who serve in combat get special pay. Officers whose specialties are engineering and science also receive special pay when they sign up for additional years of service. Incentive pay is given to officers with hazardous duties, such as work with highly toxic fuels or in explosives demolition, as well as to navigators, pilots, and flight surgeons. Officers and enlisted personnel have the same basic Air Force benefits, but officers receive extra benefits too. When they travel, they are given a monthly allowance for meals off base. Officers may continue their higher education, with partial tuition paid. Finally, they are eligible for retirement benefits after twenty years of active service.

A member of the Air Force National Guard tests a phone circuit in a technical control shelter. The National Guard is assigned to state governors, who can call on these units to preserve peace, order, and public safety.

Air Force Reserve and Air National Guard

The Air Force maintains a large number of reserve personnel. Reservists do not serve full-time but are trained and kept in readiness until they are needed. They work at regular jobs during the week and then report for military duty one weekend each month as well as an additional fifteen days each year. These reservists are trained for a specific purpose or mission and serve alongside active-duty personnel when called.

Some reservists train regularly as a unit. They are ready for combat and can be sent anywhere in the world within seventy-two hours. Some reservists do not train regularly but are called up to train when they are needed. Another group of reservists have retired

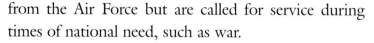

from the Air Force but are called for service during times of national need, such as war.

Those who join the Reserve often do so because they can serve in the Air Force yet can live and work as civilians when they are not involved in duties as reservists. The requirements for joining the Air Force Reserve are the same as for enlisted personnel.

The Air National Guard (ANG) is another reserve force that receives Air Force training. Over 100,000 people are in the Air National Guard. ANG units are assigned to the state governors, who can call on these units to help preserve peace, order, and public safety whenever needed. In addition, units can be called up by the president of the United States. ANG personnel are on inactive duty until called to serve.

Requirements for joining the Air National Guard are the same as for other enlisted airmen. Air Force pay and benefits are also available to ANG personnel with added benefits from the states in which they serve.

Structure of the Air Force

Air Force structure begins with the individual. Once accepted into the Air Force, the individual may become part of a *flight*, a unit of about forty-five people used for a small mission. Ten flights form a *squadron*, the basic Air Force unit, though the number of flights can change according to the mission. Two or more squadrons constitute a *wing*, around which an Air Force *base* is formed. Several wings make a *numbered air force*. Major *commands* have several numbered air forces.

Air Force Bases

An Air Force base is made up of four main groups: an operations group, which has aircrews and intelligence squadrons; a logistics group, responsible for mainte-nance and supply; a support group, made up of security forces and civil engineers; and a medical group. Each group includes officers, enlisted men and women, and civilian personnel. A base is usually under the command of a general. Bases in the United States are usually named after a hero from Air Force history, while most overseas bases are named for their geographic location.

An Air Force base is much like a town or small city, offering similar services. There is housing for officers as well as enlisted men and women. Medical care and dental care are also available at the base medical facility. Security forces, or police, and fire units ensure safety, while civil engineers maintain base roads and

The Air Force base commissary, or supermarket, is a place for military personnel to buy their food. The commissary has lower prices than a regular supermarket.

buildings. The base has a post office, a library, and a chapel for religious services.

Shopping facilities are available through a base exchange (BX) and a commissary, or base supermarket. The BX operates a retail store, automotive services, some food operations, and other businesses, depending on the size of the base. The retail store and commissary sell goods at lower prices than civilian stores.

An Air Force base also has a recreational authority that operates facilities such as a gym, bowling alley, golf course, and swimming pool. The authority offers classes on a variety of interests and hobbies, such as photography or art. It sometimes acquires discount tickets to local performances and other attractions.

Commands

The Air Force has eight major commands, each having several numbered forces. Most of the commands are located within the United States; two are overseas. Each command has a different function, but all carry out the Air Force mission to defend the United States through the use and control of air and space.

Air Combat Command (ACC)

The Air Combat Command (ACC) is located at Langley AFB in Virginia. ACC's main purpose is to organize, train, equip, and maintain combat forces critical to national security. The ACC's primary mission is to provide rapid and decisive airpower

A B-1B bomber is a stealth bomber that has the ability to fly long distances without refueling and to take off with a heavy load. The Air Combat Command at Langley AFB is responsible for maintaining these aircraft.

anywhere on earth. The command accomplishes this by means of the highly trained forces who operate the bombers, fighters, and other combat aircraft. These forces include the Air Force stealth planes, such as the B-1 and B-2 bombers, the F-117 attack fighters, and the new F-22 air-combat fighters. The ACC is also responsible for reconnaissance aircraft and rescue helicopters. ACC pilots fly more than 33,000 hours a month.

Air Mobility Command (AMC)

Another major command is the Air Mobility Command (AMC), which airlifts personnel and supplies by means of transport aircraft. This command is responsible for the aerial tankers, which refuel the transport planes, bombers, and fighters in midair, enabling them to fly thousands of miles without stopping. Aeromedical evacuation, made possible by C-9s, C-130s, and C-141s, is under the jurisdiction of AMC. This command is responsible for Air Force One, the president's plane.

From its headquarters at Scott AFB in Illinois, the AMC has provided support for operations in Bosnia, the Gulf War, Kosovo, and Somalia and for airlifting relief goods to hurricane victims. It also flew search and rescue teams to Turkey after an earthquake in August 1999.

Air Education and Training Command (AETC)

The Air Education and Training Command (AETC), headquartered at Randolph AFB in Texas, has the key mission of recruiting and training all Air Force enlisted and officer personnel, including the OTS and ROTC programs. It includes basic training, technical training, and flight training at various Air Force bases.

The AETC also provides the continuing education that is necessary for Air Force career advancement. One major unit is the Air University at Maxwell AFB in Alabama, which operates a community college program where enlistees can work toward a college degree. The Air University also offers a graduate-degree program through its Air Force Institute of Technology at Wright-Patterson AFB, Ohio (named after the Wright Brothers and a World War II hero). AETC oversees some civilian programs such as the Civil Air Patrol (CAP), the CAP cadet program, and the JROTC.

Air Force One

Air Force One, based at Andrews AFB near Washington, D.C., stands ready to fly the U.S. president anywhere, anytime. The airplane is equipped with sophisticated flight and communication systems features and is flown by experienced Air Force pilots. Although the Boeing 747 is known as the president's aircraft, any plane that carries the commander in chief can be called Air Force One.

President John F. Kennedy named the first Air Force One; Mrs. Kennedy selected its white and blue colors. During its first year of operation, Air Force One carried the assassinated president's body from Dallas to Washington. This plane is on display in the Air Force Museum at Wright-Patterson AFB, Ohio.

A student and instructor at the undergraduate navigator school of the Air Education and Training Command climb into the cockpit of a T-37 training aircraft prior to making a flight.

Air Force Materiel Command (AFMC)

The Air Force Materiel Command (AFMC) has the responsibility of researching, developing, testing, and producing advanced Air Force weapons systems. The AFMC is headquartered in Ohio at Wright-Patterson AFB along with its main research laboratory. Another AFMC test center, at Edwards AFB in California, operates the Air Force Flight Test Center. The Space and Missile Systems Center, located at Los Angeles AFB, is also under the AFMC.

Air Force Space Command (AFSPC)

The Air Force Space Command (AFSPC) has its headquarters at Peterson AFB, Colorado. The Cheyenne

The command post of the North American Air Defense Command (NORAD) Cheyenne Mountain Complex. The command post is located inside a mountain in Colorado.

Mountain Air Station Colorado, also part of Peterson AFB, is where the Command and Control (NORAD, or North American Air Defense) Squadron is based. It is actually located inside a mountain. The wings within this command test and operate worldwide missile-warning radar systems and Department of Defense satellites. AFSPC launches space satellites for military, civil, and commercial purposes from sites outside Colorado. However, NASA is the prime launch agent for nonmilitary satellites.

Air Force Special Operations Command (AFSOC)

The Air Force Special Operations Command (AFSOC) is headquartered at Hurlburt Field, Florida. This command provides specialized air-combat power to anywhere in the world at any time. These specialized forces operate the heavily armed attack helicopters, fixed-wing gunships, and heavy-lift combat helicopters. The AFSOC was involved in Desert Shield/Desert Storm operations during the Persian Gulf War. This command also assists efforts to stop the flow of narcotics into and within the United States and takes part in humanitarian efforts throughout the United States. Two special operations units have overseas bases, one in the United Kingdom and the other in Japan.

Air Force Reserve Command (AFRC)

The Air Force Reserve Command (AFRC), authorized by Congress in 1997, is the newest Air Force

The Air Force Special Operations Command uses heavily armed attack helicopters and heavy-lift combat helicopters, like the MH-53J Pave Low III. It can provide specialized air-combat power to anywhere in the world at any time.

Members of the Air Force Reserve Command 315th Aeromedical Evacuation Squadron set up a new three-tier patient litter system on a C-17 aircraft.

command. Although headquartered at Robins AFB, Georgia, it has reserve units at other command bases. Reserve units are trained to operate combat planes, airlift and rescue aircraft, and refueling tankers. They also help in aerial fire fighting and weather reconnaissance. The AFRC has three numbered air forces containing thirty-seven flying wings.

The other Air Force reserve component, the Air National Guard (ANG) provides trained personnel to the states' governors, but it reports to headquarters in Washington, DC. The ANG has eighty-eight flying wings. These forces operate the same types of aircraft that the active-duty personnel operate, with some exceptions. The ANG units also provide relief missions and do rescue work. They have been involved in operations in the Persian Gulf, Bosnia, Iraq, and Central America, among others. Along with the AFRC, this component has become increasingly important amid the downsizing of the regular Air Force.

Pacific Air Forces (PACAF)

The Air Force also has two major overseas commands. One is the Pacific Air Forces (PACAF) headquartered at Hickam AFB, Hawaii. Its mission is to plan, coordinate, and carry out air operations in the Pacific and in Asia. The PAF has nine bases: one in Hawaii and two in Alaska; one on the island of Guam in the Western Pacific; two bases in South Korea; and three bases in Japan.

United States Air Forces in Europe (USAFE)

The other overseas command is the United States Air Forces in Europe (USAFE), where the Air Force also maintains a large presence. Headquartered at Ramstein AB in Germany, this major command is responsible for providing military operations to parts of Europe, Africa, the Mediterranean, and the Middle East. It has six bases: one in Italy, two in Germany, one in Turkey, and two in the United Kingdom. The USAFE had the responsibility for planning, organizing, and carrying out JTF Shining Hope in Albania. In addition, USAFE units contributed much to the success of U.S. efforts in the Persian Gulf, Bosnia, and Kosovo.

Field Operating Agencies

The Air Force has thirty-one Field Operating Agencies (FOA) in addition to the nine major commands. These agencies have the same organizational and administrative responsibilities as major commands, but they have different missions. One field operating agency is the Air Force Center for Environmental Excellence at Brooks AFB, Texas. Its mission is to provide expertise to protect, restore, and develop the nation's environmental resources. This agency ensures that Air Force units operate within environmental laws; it is also responsible for pollution prevention and for hazardous waste cleanup at Air Force bases.

Direct Reporting Units

The Air Force also has five Direct Reporting Units (DRU) that report directly to Air Force headquarters. These units are organized in the same way as the major commands are, but they have special missions within the Air Force. Among these is the 11th Wing, located at Bolling AFB in Washington, D.C. The Air Force Band and the Air Force Honor Guard are under this wing. The Air Force Academy is another unit that reports directly to headquarters.

The United States Air Force Band

The Air Force Band is a collection of eight different musical groups:

1. Concert Band—U.S. Air Force (USAF) showcase band

2. Singing Sergeants—the official USAF chorus

3. High Flight Show Band—five vocalists who perform popular music

4. Silver Wings—country music band

5. Strolling Strings—string players who join with the Concert Band to form the USAF Chamber Orchestra and Symphony Orchestra

6. Airmen of Note—big-band jazz instrumentalists

7. Ceremonial Brass—brass players who perform at official ceremonies

8. Chamber Singers—members from the other groups who present vocal chamber music recitals

The Air Force Band, stationed at Bolling AFB near Washington, D.C., performs in this country and abroad. The groups are called "America's International Musical Ambassadors."

Department of the Air Force

The military head of the Air Force is the chief of staff, who reports to the secretary of the Air Force, a civilian. The secretary heads the Department of the Air Force, headquartered at the Pentagon. All of the commands, field operating agencies, and direct reporting units, along with the individuals working within them, make up the Department of Air Force.

The Air Force structure is part of the national military command structure. The Department of the Air

Dr. Sheila Widnall, first female secretary of the Air Force, shown here with Lieutenant General Joe Ralston just before her flight in an F-15. The secretary of the Air Force reports directly to the secretary of defense.

Force is one of the military services under the Joint Chiefs of Staff. The secretary of the Air Force reports directly to the secretary of defense.

Heading the nation's entire military structure is the commander in chief, the president of the United States. The president's position as civilian commander of the military is mandated by the U.S. Constitution. Civilian control over the military is considered fundamental to our government.

Careers in the Air Force

Air Force enlisted personnel and officers have about 150 career fields each. Many of those fields overlap, with airmen and officers working together. The greatest number of Air Force personnel is in aerospace and medical fields.

Aerospace Careers

Say "Air Force," and most people automatically think of the pilots who fly the aircraft. Nearly 18 percent of the Air Force officers are pilots. They fly many types of aircraft: bombers, fighters, attack planes, helicopters, transports, aerial tankers, reconnaissance, and test planes.

Pilots who fly the U-2 reconnaissance plane, also known as "The Dragon Lady," are somewhat less well known than others, such as bomber or fighter pilots.

Approximately one thousand pilots fly U-2s. About 40 percent of the pilots who apply qualify to fly the Dragon Lady, which looks like a giant glider, spray-painted black. This jet-powered plane soars more than 70,000 feet and is packed from nose to tail with photography equipment that gathers and processes information on enemy forces.

Flying at this altitude, the U-2 pilot must wear a pressurized space suit. A physiological support team helps with the pilot's flight preparation. These technicians maintain the space suit and help the pilot suit up. The support team inspects the suit about a half-dozen times before flight. If the space suit is damaged in any way and fails to provide the necessary protection, the pilot would die within a half minute.

The U-2 is a single-seat, single-engine, high-altitude reconnaissance aircraft. The plane soars more than 70,000 feet in the air, gathering data and transmitting it to analysts on the ground.

About an hour before flight, the pilot begins breathing 100 percent oxygen, which removes nitrogen from blood and tissues. At extreme altitudes (or depths, in the case of water), nitrogen in the blood causes "bends," or decompression sickness that can result in paralysis and death. The physiological support team monitors the pilot during oxygen intake. They also hook the pilot to the plane's life support system. Pilots cannot wear hair gel, skin lotion, or lip balm, because these products can interact with oxygen and cause spontaneous combustion.

Only one pilot can fit into the U-2, but a trained backup pilot called a mobile officer (or simply a "mobile') can fly in the place of the pilot if needed. The mobile performs the preflight check on the aircraft, because the spacesuit limits the pilot's ability to inspect the plane. Since the pilot's side vision is limited by the helmet, the mobile is also needed during landing to guide the pilot down the taxiway in order to prevent the plane's 104-foot wings from hitting the taxiway lights.

In flight, the U-2 gathers data from the earth below and transmits photos and other information to intelligence and imagery analysts at ground stations. These experts evaluate information and send it to Air Force commanders around the world.

While flying at very high altitudes, the U-2 handles well. However, the plane is sluggish at low altitudes, and landing the U-2 is a challenge. During the plane's approach, the mobile officer follows behind in a

In order to survive, U-2 pilots must wear space suits similar to this one.

ground vehicle. When the U-2 drops to about ten feet above the runway, the mobile verbally guides the pilot down to two feet by radio. Then the pilot stalls the plane, and the tail wheel (located near the plane's center of gravity) settles on the runway. According to one U-2 pilot: "Some days, you're on top of your game—dancing with the lady. Other days, you don't fly so well, and it's like fighting with a dragon to get the aircraft down."[1]

Maintenance Careers

No plane would be able to fly without maintenance technicians. Aerospace maintenance has the largest

A maintenance crew chief inspects an engine of a Galaxy aircraft prior to the plane's flight. Maintenance technicians are in high demand in the Air Force.

SWL 600 LBS

number of enlisted personnel in the Air Force, and it is one of the career fields in which people are most needed. The maintainers, as they are called, service the various types of aircraft after they land and before they take off. Maintenance technicians are well trained and take their jobs seriously.

The maintenance crews work in teams, and there are crews for each plane. When the aircraft lands, a ground crew member directs the pilot to the parking area where the plane will be serviced. The maintainers then go over the plane, examining the aircraft inside and out. They check the oil, the tires, and various other parts of the aircraft and then refuel the plane. They review the aircraft log, where the pilot or aircrew would have reported mechanical problems, if there had been any. They also ask the pilot if anything out of the ordinary occurred during the flight. The head of the maintenance team, the crew chief, is responsible for seeing that everything is done correctly. No aircraft takes off until all systems are checked and signed off by the crew chief. The lives of the pilots and aircrews depend on the men and women who maintain their planes.

Medical Careers

The medical field contains the largest number of Air Force officers and is the second largest career field for enlisted personnel. These health care providers include doctors, nurses, and medical technicians in all specialties. They work in Air Force base clinics, hospitals, and medical centers throughout the United States and abroad. Some work in aeromedical evacuation units. The medical professionals have the important charge of seeing that those who join the Air Force are kept in the best possible health. Family members of Air Force personnel also receive care from this system.

All Air Force bases provide some form of medical care, ranging from large hospitals offering a full range of services to health clinics found on smaller bases. The Air Force medical flagship hospital is Wilford Hall Medical Center, located at Lackland AFB in Texas. Home of the 59th Medical Wing, it is the largest military hospital in the United States. Wilford Hall contains 1,000 hospital beds. Every year it admits approximately 25,000 inpatients and provides services

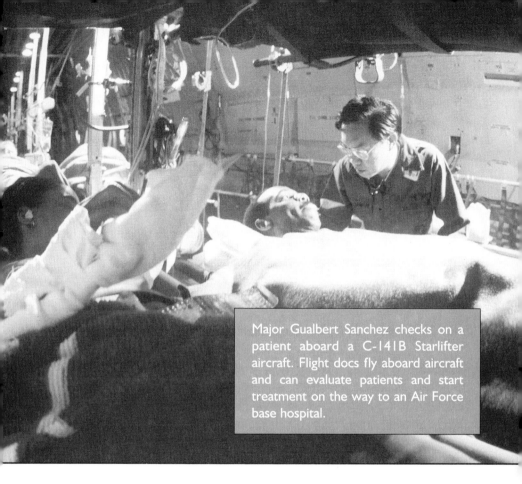

Major Gualbert Sanchez checks on a patient aboard a C-141B Starlifter aircraft. Flight docs fly aboard aircraft and can evaluate patients and start treatment on the way to an Air Force base hospital.

to more than one million outpatients a year. Almost 5,000 people work at Wilford Hall. The medical center has many specialties, such as pediatric cardiology. It also operates a special burn center and conducts medical research.

Sometimes Air Force doctors take medical care to the crew members on the flight line—the parking and service area for aircraft—rather than having people come to them in the medical center. One doctor assigned to an Air Force base in Saudi Arabia had her name painted on an F-15 as a special honor. The grateful crew chiefs dedicated the plane to the physician because of her exceptional medical skills and caring attitude toward her patients.[2]

Flight surgeons for fighter plane units have a special two-week training program called "Top Knife." (This is a play on the phrase "Top Gun," the award given to the pilot in a wing with the best record in bombing and strafing exercises.) Part of this special training requires the flight surgeon to ride as passenger in the back seat of a fighter plane on at least five or six occasions. The program is designed to give the doctors firsthand experience of the unique stresses to which the fighter pilots they treat are exposed.

One flight medical specialty is aeromedical evacuation. Aeromedical evacuation teams treat patients while they are being airlifted to hospitals. These aeromedical units serve all the U.S. military forces as well as the Department of Veterans Affairs and civilian

The Air Force uses the specially designed C-9 Nightingale for aeromedical evacuations. The C-9 features advanced medical equipment and can carry up to forty patients.

Selected Air Force Career Specialties[3]

Enlisted

- Loadmaster
- Aircrew operations
- Flight engineer
- Safety
- Survival, evasion, resistance, and escape training
- Aircrew protection
- Weather
- Manned aerospace maintenance
- Fuels
- Linguist
- Missile and space systems maintenance
- Aerospace warning and control
- Supply
- Transportation and vehicle maintenance
- Munitions and weapons
- Communications/computer systems
- Morale, welfare, recreation, and service
- USAF color guard
- Security forces
- Air traffic control
- Electrical
- Ground radio communications
- Pharmacy
- Physical therapy
- Still photos
- Imagery analysis
- Radio and television broadcasting
- Special investigator

Officer

- Fighter pilot
- Bomber navigator
- Astronaut
- Space and missile
- Intelligence
- Air combat manager
- Foreign area
- Operations support
- Operations staff officer
- Civil engineer
- Scientist
- Services
- Band
- Pathologist
- Dentist
- Public affairs
- Communications and information
- Logistician
- Flight nurse
- Flight surgeon
- Aerospace medicine specialist
- Historian
- Judge advocate (lawyer)
- Chaplain
- Instructor
- Development engineering
- Acquisition manager
- Contracting
- Financial
- Personnel

hospitals. Aeromedical units have cared for injured personnel within the United States, treated victims of terrorist bombings overseas, and airlifted U.S. prisoners of war in Bosnia. They have also picked up Russian cosmonauts and U.S. astronauts for the *Mir* space station.

For aeromedical evacuation, the Air Force uses three kinds of aircraft: the C-9 Nightingale, C-141 Starlifter, and C-130 Hercules. The C-9 is specially designed for aeromedical evacuation. This aircraft features advanced medical equipment and can carry up to forty injured or ill patients, including those on stretchers and those able to walk. The C-9's crew of eight includes a pilot, a copilot, two flight nurses, three

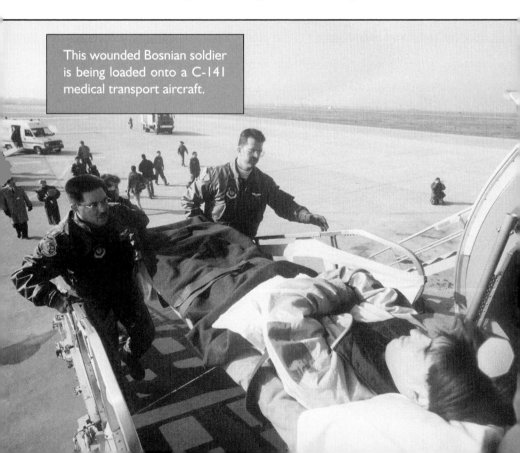

This wounded Bosnian soldier is being loaded onto a C-141 medical transport aircraft.

aeromedical technicians, and a flight mechanic. Because of critical nature of its mission, each plane also carries spare aircraft parts so that the mechanic can readily make repairs.

Medical crews highly trained in trauma and emergency care face unique problems while treating patients in the air. One example is a patient with a skull fracture. If the air pressure during flight is not the same as when the plane is on the ground, air can seep into the fracture. As a result the brain will swell, causing the death of the patient. Therefore, great care is taken to maintain proper air pressure in the plane.

The aerospace and medical fields offer but a few of the many interesting career choices for enlisted personnel and officers. The United States Air Force has a great need for well-trained, highly motivated men and women to serve in all career fields.

Women and Minorities in the Air Force

Women and members of minority groups play vital roles in today's military. The U.S. Air Force policy toward women and minorities is one of equal and just treatment. Air Force policy is "to conduct its affairs free from arbitrary discrimination, according to United States laws, and to provide equal opportunity and treatment for all members irrespective of their age, color, national origin, race, ethnic group, religion, or sex."[1]

This nondiscrimination policy applies to recruitment, training, and career advancement for all Air Force personnel. But this was not always so for women and minorities.

Women in the Air Force

Women have always served this country during wartime. Female nurses, for instance, have performed nobly during all America's wars. But until World War II, women's roles in the military were mostly supportive, or auxiliary.

During World War I, women aviators who applied to fly in combat were denied, but they found other ways to help. Marjorie Stinson, known as the "Flying Schoolmarm," trained American and Canadian cadets at her flying school in San Antonio, Texas. In 1915, Georgia "Tiny" Broadwick became the first person to demonstrate the parachute to government officials. General George Scriven, chief of the U.S. Army's aviation bureau, was impressed and congratulated Broadwick on her parachute jump.[2]

During the 1920s and 1930s, numerous women inspired by the famous aviators—Charles Lindbergh, Amelia Earhart, Jacqueline Cochran, and others—took to the skies and earned pilot's licenses. The largest single group of women fliers became licensed through the government's Civilian Pilot Training Program (CPTP), which began in 1939.

Under this program, students were trained at local colleges and universities in the United States and Puerto Rico. Colleges provided books and instructors for ground school; local airports provided the flight instructors. Every tenth slot was designated for a woman. By the time the CPTP converted to the War Training Service (restricted to men) in 1941, over 2,500 women had earned their private pilot's licenses.

When war broke out in Europe in 1939, two notable women aviators, Nancy Harkness Love and

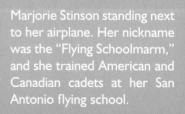

Marjorie Stinson standing next to her airplane. Her nickname was the "Flying Schoolmarm," and she trained American and Canadian cadets at her San Antonio flying school.

Jacqueline "Jackie" Cochran, thought that female pilots could make valuable contributions if the United States ultimately entered the war. Each presented a different plan to Army aviation officials.

In 1940, Love proposed that the small group of women pilots holding commercial licenses deliver or ferry military aircraft. Jackie Cochran proposed a military flight-training program for women who held private licenses. General H. "Hap" Arnold reviewed the two plans but turned them down because he thought women pilots were not needed at the time. He also believed that such a program would generate controversy.

General Arnold suggested that Cochran select a number of women pilots to help the British Transport Auxiliary. Cochran selected twenty-four highly skilled pilots, and for eighteen months, they helped deliver planes in Great Britain. One pilot, Cochran's personal secretary, was killed when her propeller blade came off.

When the United States entered World War II, planes rolled off assembly lines. With most of the male military pilots serving combat duty, fliers were desperately needed to ferry planes from the manufacturers to military bases or to port cities for shipment overseas.

In September 1942, General Arnold approved both Love's and Cochran's plans for civilian women pilots. Love's elite group, the Women's Auxiliary Ferry Squadron (WAFS) started delivering planes, while Cochran began her women's training program— almost identical to that of the male cadets. The

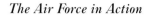

Colonel Jacqueline "Jackie" Cochran
(1908–1980)
Aviator, Director of WASP

Born into poverty, Jackie Cochran became a successful businesswoman and a famous aviator. Before 1940, she set three speed records, set one world altitude record, and won the Harmon Trophy three times. She was the creator and director of the Women Airforce Service Pilots (WASP) during World War II. In 1948, she was promoted to lieutenant colonel.

Cochran became the first woman to break the sound barrier in 1953. She flew the dangerous Lockheed F-104 Starfighter when she was 52 years old. At her death in 1980, she held more speed, altitude, and distance records than any pilot in history. The Air Force Academy has a permanent Jacqueline Cochran display in Colorado Springs.

Women's Flying Training Detachment (WFTD), Cochran's group, started training in Houston, Texas. The program was later moved to Avenger Field in Sweetwater, Texas—the only all-woman military base in U.S. history. The women pilots were restricted to flying within the United States.

The two civilian groups finally merged in August 1943 to become the Women Airforce Service Pilots (WASP), under the direction of Jackie Cochran, with Love in charge of the ferry pilots. Cochran expanded the WASP program to include towing targets for gunnery practice, flight-testing planes, instruction, and other aviation duties.

By the time the WASPs were disbanded in December 1944, 1,074 civilian women pilots had flown 60 million miles in every type of military aircraft made. Thirty-eight WASPs died in service to their country. One was Chinese American Hazel Ying Lee, who perished when her pursuit plane collided with another plane while making a runway approach.

The Army Air Force also had a program for women. In May 1942, Congress passed the Women's Army Auxiliary Corps (WAAC) with Oveta Culp Hobby as director. Although they did not pilot planes, the WAACs had an air unit that monitored radios and radar for signs of air attacks. In July 1943, the name was changed to the Women's Army Corps (WAC), and the women were given military status.

In June 1948, Congress passed the Women's Armed Forces Integration Act, giving active-duty and reserve status to women in all the military branches. Former WASPs did not receive full military recognition until 1977.

The WAC was changed to the Women in the Air Force (WAF) in 1948. However, the WAFs had certain restrictions placed on them. The number of women was limited to no more than 2 percent of the total air forces. Women in the Air Force could not rise above the level of lieutenant colonel (with one exception: one woman in each military service was permitted to advance to colonel). Women were paid less than their male counterparts, and, if they married or had children, they had to leave the military. The WAF existed as a separate but unequal organization until 1967.

A small number of women served in the Korean War, mostly in nursing or support roles. Women joined in increasing numbers during the Vietnam War.

With most male pilots serving in combat, women were urgently needed to perform other aviation duties during World War II.

Several former WASPs served in Vietnam. As the war continued, they were assigned to higher positions within the Air Force commands. One former WASP, a lieutenant colonel, served in Vietnam. Important developments took place for Air Force women during the 1960s. In 1965, President Lyndon Johnson signed Executive Order 11375, prohibiting discrimination based on sex. In 1967, the 2 percent ceiling was lifted, as were the limitations on rank. In 1969, Colonel Jeanne Holms advanced to brigadier general. That same year the ROTC program began admitting women for officer training.

Many changes occurred in the 1970s. Pregnant women were no longer discharged. In 1976, ten women lieutenants entered pilot training, and the Air Force Academy first admitted women cadets. Four years later, 157 women graduated from the Academy. Of that first class, seven women became command officers; four became special assistants to the secretary of the Air Force; and one, astronaut Susan Helms, flew on three shuttle missions. Another became co-pilot on Air Force Two (the vice president's plane).

In the next decade, Air Force women were involved in important military operations. They were among the forces sent to invade Grenada in the Caribbean in 1983. In 1989, 170 women were part of Operation Just Cause in Panama, where they served as members of airlift crews and air tankers.

During the Persian Gulf War, over 40,000 military women participated in Operations Desert Shield and

The first ten female officers to graduate from the Air Force Undergraduate Pilot Training Program in front of a T-38 training aircraft. It wasn't until 1976 that women were allowed to enter the pilot training program.

Desert Storm. Some 12,500 Air Force women served in transport and medical evacuations. A few flew tankers and cargo planes to Saudi Arabia, while many worked in aircraft maintenance.

In 1991, Congress repealed the law that excluded women from serving in combat areas (only ground combat positions remain closed to women). Two years later, women pilots climbed into fighter plane cockpits as pilots. They had already been flying airplanes as instructors and as aggressor pilots in mock air-combat exercises. In 1995, Air Force Lieutenant Colonel Eileen Collins piloted the space shuttle Discovery. She became the first female mission commander in 1999.

In October 1997, the memorial for Women in Military Service for America was dedicated at Arlington National Cemetery, Virginia. This memorial honors the 1.8 million women who have served in the military from the Revolutionary War to the present. Secretary of Defense William S. Cohen stated at the memorial dedication: "We don't allow women in service as a social favor; we do not train women in the name of a noble social experiment. Today, women in uniform are part of the national security of the United States, and this isn't a modern nicety, it's a military necessity."[3]

Major Carol A. DiBattiste
Undersecretary of the Air Force, 1999–2000

As undersecretary, the Honorable Carol A. DiBattiste was responsible for the actions of the Air Force on behalf of the secretary of the Air Force. She also was acting secretary in the secretary's absence.

DiBattiste enlisted in the Air Force in 1971, serving as a recruiter and finance specialist. In 1976, she was commissioned upon finishing Officer Training School. After completing two law degrees, she served as a circuit prosecutor and judge advocate at Air Force bases. She was also a faculty member of the Air Force Judge Advocate General School.

DiBattiste served in the Defense and Justice departments before her 1999 appointment as undersecretary. She returned to civilian life as a lawyer in January 2001.

African Americans in the Air Force

African Americans and members of other minority groups also had problems being accepted in the military. The first African-American aviator, Eugene Jacques Bullard, chose to leave the United States for greater opportunities abroad. As a young man, he joined the French Foreign Legion and was later trained as a pilot during World War I. He scored two kills and became a French national hero; however, Bullard remained unknown in his native America.[4] Though Bullard was the first African-American aviator, he was not licensed. Bessie Coleman became the first licensed African-American pilot in 1927.

In 1941, President Franklin D. Roosevelt signed Executive Order 8802, which prohibited discrimination based on race, color, creed, or national origin in government or in defense industries. But it would be many years before African Americans would be accepted as equals in the military.

Over one million African Americans served in the armed forces during World War II. Among the most famous were the Tuskegee Airmen. In 1940, the Tuskegee Institute in Alabama hired Charles "Chief" Anderson to develop a civilian pilot training program for African Americans. At the time, he was the only African American in the country to hold a commercial pilot's license.

In 1941, the War Department established a flight school for African Americans at Tuskegee, with Anderson as instructor. West Point graduate and pilot

Benjamin O. Davis, Jr., also taught at Tuskegee. When war broke out, then-Colonel Davis was given command of four hundred African-American fighter pilots.

One group—the 99th Fighter Squadron—fought in aerial combat over Europe, including Sicily, and North Africa. The squadron escorted and protected heavy bombers, and never lost a bomber to enemy attack. The white crewmen on the bombers named the

General Benjamin O. Davis, Jr.
(1912–)
Commander of Tuskegee Airmen

Benjamin Davis, Jr., son of the first African-American brigadier general in the U.S. Army, was born in Washington, D.C, and grew up in Tuskegee, Alabama. Davis attended West Point, where he endured four years during which his peers spoke to him only when necessary for official business.

Davis learned to fly at Tuskegee, his first assignment. During World War II, he commanded the Tuskegee Airmen and earned the Distinguished Flying Cross. He also served in Korea and Vietnam. Davis expected excellence from the men he commanded.

In 1970, he retired as major general, then worked with the Transportation Department. In a 1998 White House ceremony, President Bill Clinton awarded Davis his fourth star.

fighter pilots the "Redtail Devils" because of the red paint on their aircraft tails. The Germans called them the "Black Birdmen." The enemy feared and respected these pilots.

Other squadrons made up of African Americans included the 100th, 301st, and the 302nd. The three formed the 332nd Fighter Group. These fighter pilots destroyed enemy ground targets and engaged in aerial combat. Sixty-six African-American pilots were killed, and thirty-two were taken prisoners of war. They earned 150 Distinguished Flying Crosses and Legions of Merit, among other awards.

African-American women also enlisted in the military. When the WAAC was formed, the War

The Tuskegee Airmen, the first African-American fighter pilots, served with distinction in World War II.

Department made a commitment to recruit and train African-American women. Director Hobby fully supported this. Out of the first class of 440 WAACs, eight African-American women were officer candidates. However, Director Hobby ran into opposition from African-American leaders who feared these women would be put in segregated units, as were African-American men in the military. Their fears came true. In addition, many African-American women were assigned as cooks and postal clerks, regardless of their skills and training. About four thousand African-American women served in the WAAC and the WAC.

One civilian African-American pilot, Janet Waterford Bragg Harmon, applied to the WASP. While Director Cochran recognized Harmon's flying abilities, she discouraged her because she feared an African-American woman would encounter problems at Army air bases. Instead, Harmon became a flight instructor at the Tuskegee Institute.

In 1948, President Truman signed Executive Order 9998, ordering integration of all the armed forces of the United States. Though integration was accomplished, acceptance of integration did not occur until years later.

As the number of African Americans in the Air Force increased, so did their mortality rate. Approximately 3,100 African American in the U.S. armed forces died in the Korean War. In Vietnam, more than 5,600 African Americans were killed in combat.

The 1960s witnessed the outbreak of civil rights protests in America, and in 1964, Congress passed the Civil Rights Act. However, it wasn't until the 1970s that the Air Force went through its worst period of racial problems. In May 1971, rioting took place at Travis AFB, California, in which more than two hundred airmen fought over a three-day period. African Americans complained about discrimination in assignments, among other problems. The rioting sent shock waves through the Air Force and the Department of Defense. The Pentagon launched an investigation, which concluded that there had been a breakdown between base leadership and its African-American airmen.

General Daniel "Chappie" James, Jr.
(1920–1978)
Fighter Pilot, Four-Star General

Chappie James was the first African American to become a four-star general in the Air Force. During his military career he was an articulate spokesman for the Air Force.

Although one of the Tuskegee Airmen, General James did not see combat action until Korea, where he flew over one hundred missions. He flew over sixty combat missions in Vietnam.

During the remaining ten years of his military career, James was commander of Wheelus AFB in Libya, worked in Public Affairs at the Pentagon, was vice commander of Military Airlift Command, and headed the North American Air Defense Command.

General Lloyd W. "Fig" Newton
African-American Air Force Commander

General Newton was born in Ridgeland, South Carolina. He entered the ROTC program at Tennessee State University, where he graduated with a bachelor of science degree in aviation education.

He flew 269 combat missions during the Vietnam War and received many awards. He was later a member of the Air Force's precision-flying squadron, the Thunderbirds. General Newton is a command pilot with more than four thousand flying hours.

During his career, he commanded three wings and an air division, as well as heading the Air Education and Training Command. He also held numerous staff positions and was an Air Force liaison officer with the U.S. House of Representatives.

A month later the Defense Race Relations Institute was established to address concerns. As a result, the first Social Actions office opened at Patrick AFB, Florida. Later, others were formed. The role of these offices was to educate members of the Air Force so as to prevent discrimination.

Today, Military Equal Opportunity offices exist throughout the Air Force. They handle issues such as sexual harassment and discrimination complaints related to national origin as well as racism. In addition, the Air Force discusses equal opportunity treatment in special briefings at the beginning of enlisted and officer training.

Major John W. Adams goes over some correspondence with Training Specialist Technical Sergeant Mazie Sanders. Today the U.S. Air Force is committed to equal opportunity.

Recent events show how the status of African Americans in the Air Force has improved. In 1989, General Colin Powell was appointed Chairman of the Joint Chiefs of Staff, the highest military rank ever achieved by an African American; in 2001, after retiring from the Air Force, Powell was appointed United States secretary of state. Major General Marcie Harris earned her rank in 1995, becoming the first African-American woman to do so. In 1997, Medals of Honor were awarded to seven Tuskegee Airmen: Vernon Baker, Edward Carter, Jr., John Fox, Ruben Rivers, Willy James, Jr., Charles Thomas, and George Watson. Only Vernon Baker was alive to receive his medal.

Other Minorities

Individuals from ethnic minority groups such as Native Americans and Asian Americans have also joined the Air Force to pursue educational and career opportunities. In addition, many Hispanics have had important but little-known roles in the Air Force and in aviation. ("Hispanic" is a term for people whose native language is Spanish, who have a Spanish surname, or who come from any of the twenty Spanish American countries.) For example, most aviation enthusiasts know of Amelia Earhart's contributions, yet few know that one of her flight instructors was John Montijo, a Hispanic.

During World War II, Captain Michael Brezas downed twelve enemy aircraft. He earned the Air Medal with eleven oak leaf clusters, the Distinguished Flying Cross, and the Silver Star. Lieutenant General Manuel J. Asensio served as staff air engineer in Asia, where he developed methods for airlifting heavy construction equipment. Asensio also oversaw the building of seventeen air

Major General Charles H. Perez
Logistics Commander

Major General Perez was born in Cuba. After receiving a bachelor of science degree in chemistry in 1968, he entered Air Force Officer Training School. Perez earned a master's degree in systems and logistics at the Air Force Institute of Technology. While serving in Vietnam, Perez earned a Bronze Star and other awards. Perez was promoted to major general in 1996.

His last assignment was commander of Oklahoma City Air Logistics Center at Tinker AFB, Oklahoma. He was responsible for providing worldwide logistics support for Air Force weapons systems. Major General Charles H. Perez retired from the Air Force in 1999.

bases in the South Atlantic. He was awarded the Air Medal for many dangerous low-level flights over enemy territory. Dr. Hector Garcia was also a combat hero, who worked for Hispanic rights for fifty years.

In Korea, Cuban-born American Colonel Manuel J. Hernandez flew 125 combat missions with over 14 kills. Another Cuban-American, Major General Charles Perez, was a decorated Vietnam veteran.

Each year the Air Force celebrates National Hispanic Heritage Month (September 15–October 15) at its bases. Since 1972, the Image Inc. Meritorious Service Award has been given yearly to Hispanics who have made significant contributions within the military. Many Air Force personnel have been among the recipients of these awards.

Leaders at the highest levels of military command believe that bias and bigotry are harmful to job and career performance. The military is convinced that teamwork—based on mutual trust and respect for all individuals—is vital to defending the United States. To this end Air Force has worked to stamp out bigotry, racism, and discrimination within its ranks.

The Air Force affirms the belief of General Benjamin Davis, Jr., who said, "The future of this nation is largely dependent on how Americans treat each other."[5]

The Future of the Air Force

From their early beginnings, the air forces of the United States have evolved in response to change. Now in the twenty-first century, the Air Force not only responds to changes that it encounters, it actually attempts to anticipate such changes and plan for them. The Air Force in the future will respond even more quickly to changes around the globe.

A part of the Air Force global response is the expeditionary aerospace force that is trained and prepared to act quickly when crisis situations occur abroad. The Joint Task Force (JTF) Shining Hope operation in Albania is an example of how the expeditionary aerospace force works. The Air Force achieved this quick response by the way it organized, trained, and equipped its forces.

The Air Force plans to achieve an even faster global response in the future. It will do this by creating ten forces consisting of fighter, bomber, and mobility wings. The wings include Air Force personnel, aircraft, and weapons.[1] These highly trained wings will be on call to respond quickly to an international crisis. The Aerospace Expeditionary Forces Center at Langley AFB in Virginia is responsible for the management of these rapid-response forces.[2]

Technology plays a major role in the Air Force's plans for quick global response. In addition to stealth B-1 and B-2 bombers and F-117 fighters, the Air Force plans to use even more stealth aircraft. The stealth F-22 Raptor fighter is a hundred times more difficult to detect on radar than the F-117. It is intended to replace the F-15 Eagle and the F-16 air combat fighter. Each F-22 is estimated to cost $178 million, and the B-2 costs about $2 billion.

Also included in the technology of the future are new missiles and satellites. Specially designed planes now equipped with laser missiles can shoot down enemy rockets hundreds of miles away. New communication, reconnaissance, and weather satellites will not only be used in warfare but will also benefit people in this country and around the world. Information provided by these satellites will continue to be shared with other nations on a limited basis.

The United States Air Force will continue joint operations with other nations around the world, particularly with our military allies in Europe, who make

The Air Force has developed the stealth F-22 Raptor to eventually replace the F-15 Eagle and the F-16 fighter. The F-22 is a hundred times more difficult to detect on radar than the F-117. These aircraft cost an estimated $178 million each.

up the North Atlantic Treaty Organization, or NATO. The Air Force will also conduct more joint operations with the other U.S. military services. Although joint operations take great planning and coordination, they are more cost-effective than operations undertaken alone.

Air Force personnel are an important part of the expeditionary aerospace forces. In the future, the Air Force will need more men and women with scientific and technical expertise. Such highly skilled people are needed to operate high-tech systems found in aircraft, communications systems, missiles, and satellites. In 1998, Air Force Chief of Staff General Michael E. Ryan said, "We must prepare our people for the uncertainty of the future . . . since it is they who will lead our expeditionary aerospace forces in the future."[3]

Reflecting the society from which they come, Air Force personnel will be even more diverse in the future. The Air Force will rely on more women and minorities to serve. It will continue to recruit women and minorities and—based on their individual merit—advance them into leadership positions.

With its expeditionary aerospace force, the United States Air Force is ready to respond to a future of rapid changes. But the Air Force core values—"integrity first, service before self and excellence in all we do"[4]—remain true and constant.

Chapter Notes

Chapter 1. The Mission of Today's Air Force

1. Joe Bela, "JTF Shining Hope lifeline for Kosovar refugees," *Air Force News*, April 20, 1999, pp. 2–3.

2. Mike Young. "Camp Hope soon empty," *U.S. Forces in Europe News Service*, June 29, 1999, p. 2.

3. Hardy Sellers and Robert Shindel, *Leadership Studies* (Maxwell AFB, Ala.: HQ AFOATS/CR, n.d.), p. 596.

4. United States Air Force, "Air Force Junior Reserve Officer Training Corps," Fact Sheet #99-03 (Maxwell AFB, Ala.: HQ Air University Public Affairs, July 1999).

5. "History of the CAP," *Civil Air Patrol Information Page*, n.d., <http://www.geocities.com/ofcrmulder/index .html> (June 1, 2001).

6. "Indiana, New Jersey cadets win CAP National Competitions," *Air Force News*, January 9, 1998, p. 2.

Chapter 2. History of the Air Force

1. Stephen L. McFarland, *A Concise History of the U.S. Air Force* (Maxwell AFB, Ala.: Air Force History and Museums Program, 1997), p. 2.

2. Walter J Boyne, *Beyond the Wild Blue: A History of the U.S. Air Force* (New York: St. Martin's Press, 1997), p. 12.

3. McFarland, p. 5.

4. B. Chance Saltzman, *Introduction to the United States Air Force* (Maxwell AFB, Ala.: Airpower Research Institute, 1999), p. 67.

5. Stephen Ambrose, *D-Day, June 6, 1944: The Climactic Battle of World War II* (New York: Simon & Schuster, 1994), p. 198.

6. Angela Butchko and Mark Hiatt, eds. *The Foundations of the United States Air Force* (Maxwell AFB, Ala.: HQ AFOATS/CR, n.d.), p. 122.

7. William Stueck, *The Korean War: An International History* (Princeton, N.J.: Princeton University Press, 1995), p. 3.

Chapter 3. Joining the Air Force

1. U.S. Air Force, "Technical Training School," *Student Handbook* (Maxwell AFB, Ala.: 331st Recruiting Squadron, n.d.), p. 5.

2. United States Air Force, "Air Force Reserve Officer Training Corps," Fact Sheet #99-02, (Maxwell AFB, Ala.: HQ Air University Public Affairs, July 1999), p. 1.

3. Air Force Academy, *United States Air Force Academy Catalog* (Colorado Springs, Colo.: U.S. Air Force Academy, n.d.), p. 5.

Chapter 5. Careers in the Air Force

1. Teresa Kaye, "Dancing with a Dragon Lady," *Air Force News*, February 8, 1999, p. 1.

2. Nancy Graham, "F-15 dedicated to flight surgeon," *Air Force News*, February 16, 1999, pp. 1–2.

3. Air Force Personnel Center, "Career Field Breakdown," *The Book 2000 Airman Magazine*, January 2000, pp. 1–5.

Chapter 6. Women and Minorities in the Air Force

1. Angela Butchko and Mark Hiatt, eds., *The Foundations of the United States Air Force* (Maxwell AFB, Ala.: HQ AFOATS/CR, n.d.), p. 64.

2. Claudia Oakes, *United States Women in Aviation Through World War I* (Washington, D.C.: Smithsonian Institution Press, 1978), p. 17.

3. Tammy Cournoyer, "America dedicates memorial to its service women," *Air Force News*, October 21, 1997, p. 2.

4. *Air Force News*, "First black aviator," February 16, 1996.

5. Catherine Reef, *Benjamin Davis, Jr.* (Frederick, Md.: Twenty-First Century Books), 1992, p. 11.

Chapter 7. The Future of the Air Force

1. "Leading Edge: Expeditionary Forces for the New Millennium," *Airman*, January 2000, p. 10.

2. "Leading Edge: Expeditionary Aerospace Force Facts," *Airman*, January 2000, p. 11.

3. "Warrior Week," *U.S. Air Force Basic Military Training Page*, January 28, 2000, <http://www.lackland.af.mil/737trg/737web/warrior/default.htm>.

4. Hardy Sellers and Robert Shindel, *Leadership Studies* (Maxwell AFB, Ala.: HQ AFOATS/CR, n.d.), p. 596.

Glossary

air commands—Large Air Force sections made up of wings and numbered air forces.

airlift—A system of transporting people or cargo by aircraft.

arms—Weapons.

auxiliary—A support group helping the Air Force; the Civil Air Patrol is an auxiliary group.

basic training—First training for enlisted personnel after reporting for duty.

BX—Base exchange; provides the shopping facilities on an air base.

CAP—Civil Air Patrol; a civilian auxiliary of the Air Force.

corps—A separate branch of the military having a special function, such as the Signal Corps of the U.S. Army.

court-martial—A trial of a member of the armed forces, held in a military court.

deterrence—A method of preventing war by having enough military force to convince the enemy not to make war.

dogfight—An aerial battle in which pilots try to shoot each other down.

expeditionary force—A military force that can be quickly sent abroad.

flight line—The parking and service area for aircraft.

flight simulator—A training device that mimics, or simulates, the sensations and techniques of flying.

instrument flying—Flying and navigating with the aid of the plane's instruments when visibility is limited.

joint operation—A military venture conducted by units of two or more armed forces of the same nation.

JROTC—Junior Reserve Officer Training Corps; a program conducted in high schools.

logistics—The science of obtaining, taking care of, and transporting military goods and people.

materiel—Supplies and equipment used by the military.

military—Relating to a country's armed forces.

mission—A specific combat assignment given to a unit or an individual; can also be a single combat flight by an aircraft or a group of airplanes.

munitions—Weapons and ammunition.

operation—A series of steps made in carrying out a major military plan.

ordnance—Supplies such as weapons and ammunition.

OTS—Officer Training School.

reconnaissance—An inspection or survey of an enemy's position.

Reserve—A trained force that is kept in readiness until needed.

ROTC—Reserve Officer Training Corps; a program conducted at colleges.

sortie—One flight by one aircraft.

squadron—Basic Air Force unit made up of ten flights.

stealth—A type of technology that reduces the chances that aircraft or missiles can be detected by radar.

strafe—To fly low and fire at close range.

strategic—A large long-range plan; strategic forces have the capability and range to carry war to the enemy's homeland; includes heavy bombers and ballistic missiles capable of carrying nuclear weapons.

tactical—Smaller scale action (than a strategic plan) carried out with an immediate or limited end; fighters are tactical aircraft.

wing—Fundamental working Air Force unit that consists of two or more mission squadrons in combat, airlift, or flight training; an Air Force base is built around a wing.

Further Reading

Buchanan, Doug. *Women in Air & Space*. Broomall, Pa.: Chelsea House, 1998.

Hansen, Ole Steen. *Aircraft*. Chatham, N.J.: Raintree Steck-Vaughn, 1998.

Harris, Jacqueline L. *The Tuskegee Airmen: Black Heroes of World War II*. Parsippany, N.J.: Silver Burdett Press, 1995.

Holden, Henry. *Air Force Aircraft*. Berkeley Heights, N.J.: Enslow Publishers, 2001.

Hole, Dorothy. *Air Force and You*. Parsippany, N.J.: Silver Burdett Press, 1993.

Kent, Zachary. *World War I: "The War to End Wars."* Springfield, N.J.: Enslow Publishers, Inc., 1994.

McGuire, Nina, and Sandra Wallus Sammons. *Jacqueline Cochran, America's Fearless Aviator*. Lake Buena Vista, Fla.: Tailored Tours Publications, 1997.

Nelson, Pete, and Jack W. Brehm. *That Others May Live: The True Story of a P.J., a Member of America's Most Daring Rescue Force*. New York: Crown Publishing, 2000.

O'Grady, Scott. *Basher Five-Two: The True Story of F-16 Fighter Pilot Captain Scott O'Grady*. New York: Doubleday, 1997.

Reef, Catherine. *Benjamin Davis, Jr.* New York: Twenty-First Century Books, 1995.

Stein, R. Conrad. *World War II in Europe: America Goes to War*. Springfield, N.J.: Enslow Publishers, 1994.

———. *World War II in the Pacific: Remember Pearl Harbor*. Springfield, N.J.: Enslow Publishers, 1994.

Sullivan, George E. *Famous Air Force Fighters*. New York: Putnam, 1990.

Internet Addresses

Air Force Link Page
<http://www.af.mil/>

United States Air Force Academy Page
<http://www.usafa.af.mil/>

Air Force Reserve Page
<http://www.afreserve.com/>

Air National Guard Page
<http://www.goang.af.mil/>

Index